OASIS ONE: Front Matter

Required by lore
Poetic license included

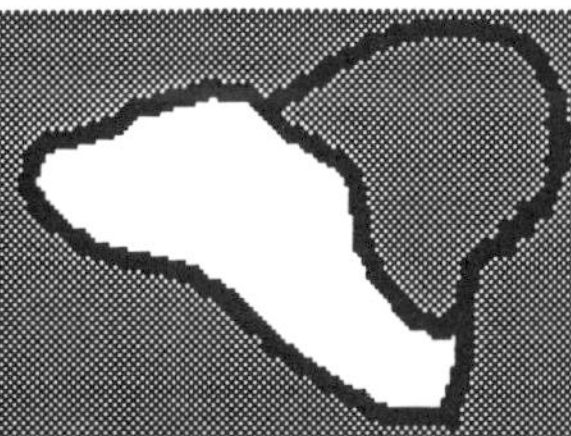

THAT'S QUITE NICE...

DID YOU DO IT?

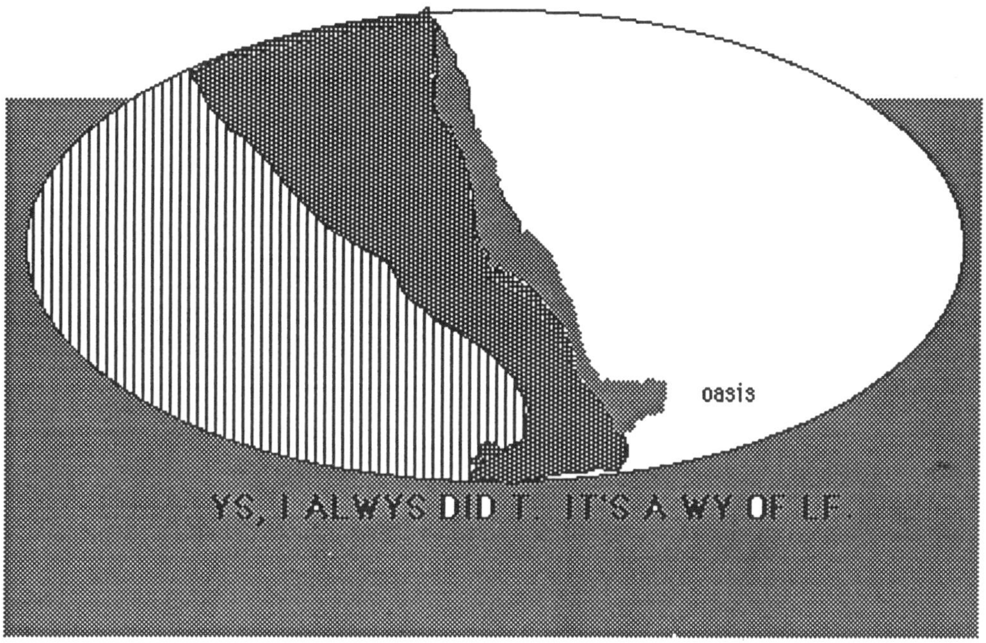

Fortunes

to go

FORTUNES

TO GO

+16,000,000 CUSTOMIZED FORTUNES

BY

Sheindeleh

> "I never met a fortune I didn't like. I never met a fortune that didn't like me back".
> Sheindeleh

ESTMOR PRESS
New York

Write to: Estmor Press, P.O. Box 10985, Staten Island N.Y. 10301

Library of Congress Cataloging-in-Publication Data

Sheindeleh

Fortunes To Go (16,000,000+ Customized Fortunes)
1. Fortunes 2. Interactive fortunes 3. Blind Sight(Braille-sighted collaborative fortunes) 4. Graphics 5. Language fortunes 6. Music & song fortunes 7. Paradoxes 8. Bromides 9. Poetic fortunes with graphics.10. Oases I. Title
FORTUNES TO GO (16,000,000+ CUSTOMIZED FORTUNES)
Library of Congress Catalog Card Number: 98-73006
ISBN 0-9665506-0-9 Hard Cover edition
ISBN 0-9665506-1-7 PBK
Printed in the United States of America
First Edition

12345678910

COMIC DRAWINGS (INNER COVERS) BY RALPH BAEZ

BOOK DESIGN AND DRAWINGS BY SHEINDELEH

COVER DESIGNS BY SHEINDELEH

DEDICATED

to my parents (for the invisible gifts they left in the future.)

to Music and other muses who held my hand during hard times

to neighbors and friends who did the translations and transliterations of the languages.

To Fran Liebowitz of the Lighthouse for her help in making the Braille enclosures a reality.

To the world
we are all connected

(trompe-l'oeil, une tromperie)

To Marty who found me my dream house.

To Charles & Ann who sold me the house and left1000 wonderful vibrations behind.

To YOU

the light gatherers and the light givers who share their best words with others.

Sheindeleh

Stephen Mihalic, a special thanks for the wisest words about love that recycle into a healing presence.

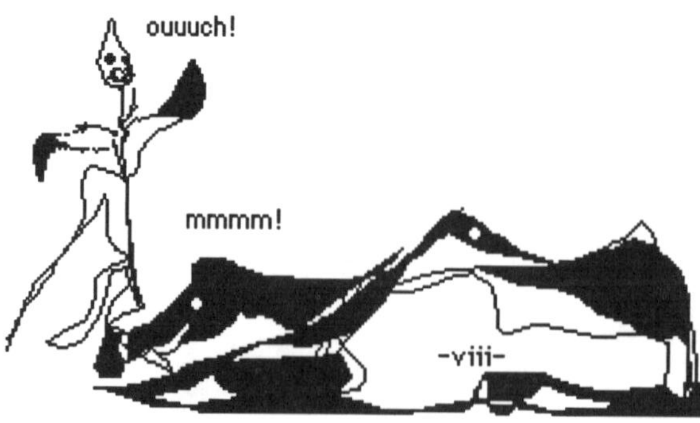
ouuuch!
mmmm!

PREFACE

Read a fortune
to feel fortunate.
Light hearted and directional.
this fortune,
this message of hope,
this confirmation of change.
this love letter
to you
Lifts the spirit with its brevity,
Its fairy tale wisdom
You Tarzan
You Jane
Fortune, your vine.
Swing yourself
Amid fields of rainbows
Fill yourself with innocent joy
Return home lightheaded
Your spirit. Like star
to Wish upon
Recall

Sheindeleh
October, 1997

TO THE 'FORTUNE' HUNTER

There are several languages included in FORTUNES TO GO Among them, Braille, Music and Obschizzo (an invented language).

NO TRANSLATION IS GIVEN. The reason: That you may connect yourself to a new friend who will translate for you.

Talk with a blind person who reads braille.

Talk with a musician who reads music.

Talk with an Arabic, French, Jewish, Korean, Spanish, or Portuguese speaking person.

The sound and connection with another, extends use of the fortune. When these folk translate they add the flavor of their culture.

To top it off ask for an English to English translation by everyone. It may surprise you.

Sheindeleh

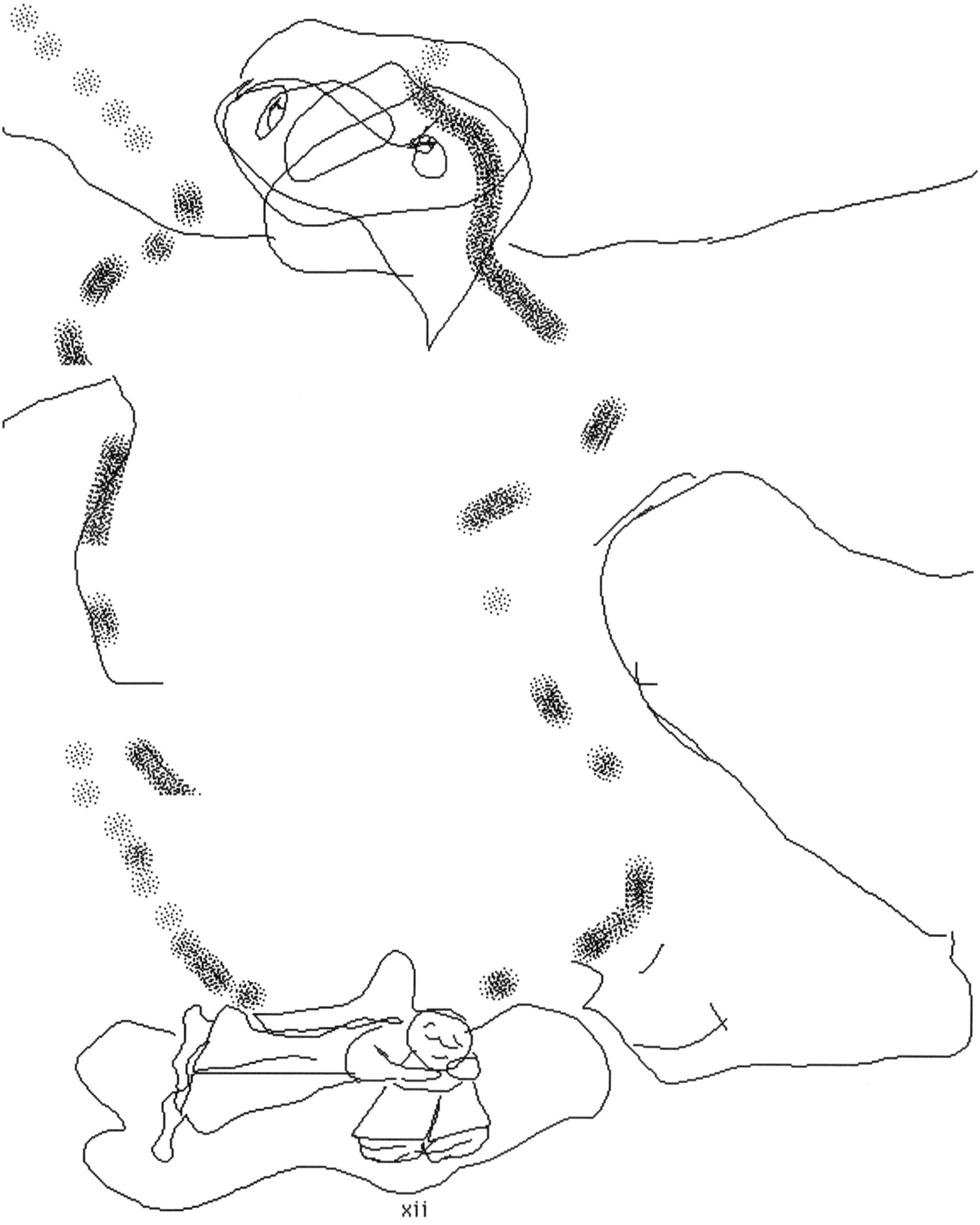

FORWARD FROM MY COMPANION

DEAR READER,
Tonight at dinner I heard a voice dictating in my head. It said all these things you are about to read. I wasn't focused on writing. This manifestation of the underlying book seems to have developed its own voice and sensibilities.
The book wants to speak to You the Reader. Sheindeleh 4/17/97

I am the book.
I am your book.
I am always here to comfort you.
Hold me embrace me turn to me.
I will not fail you.
When your sadness feels inconsolable I will console you. When no one understands - come to me. When no one listens hold me, open me up.
You will find strength in my words (the fortunes, the bromides, the songs)
Each oasis has special gifts chosen for you.
Drink up the sounds. Breathe in the love.
Explore the visions set in the images
and in a little while you will reach your sacred soul.
I am the book.
I am yours.
Turn to the Interactive pages
where you can tell me anything,
ask me anything, feel it all.
Choose the words you need to explain, cry or laugh as you will.
Allow me the privilege to twist and turn to find the correct medicine
you need to dress your wounds, rub away the mud, kiss your eyes so they open in innocent wonder.

I am your book. Every moment of every day forever.
I will not fail you
In your confusions
and in your glad moments
and in your philosophic moods
I have the food to nourish and heal each side of your spirit
your humor
your loneliness
your gentleness,
your desires to grow.
I am your book.
There are 8 oases in me. I will meet you in whichever one you desire.
All you need do is go there.
When you talk I will listen. If you listen I will talk.
I am your book.
Together we will see which aspects of life to change, which to appreciate, which to laugh at, which to ignore, which to understand better, which are falsehoods.
I am your book.
I love you every moment of every day, forever.
I will not fail you.
When you need me I am here.
I am your book.
Stay joyful and calm. The vicissitudes of life pass on.

TABLE OF CONTÉNT

At the Table of Conténtment, all dishes taste delicious. Help yourself to most or least. Each Oasis is a feast. Your table mates, disguised as you, tickle away old points of view. Question them to heart's content, knowing they are heaven sent. Chat a bit, laugh a lot, your heart rejoices on the spot. There's much to chew and much to see. Un vrai bon appétit, mes beaux amis.

<u>OASIS 2</u> Pictures with Words

A picture is worth a thousand words
A word creates a thousand pictures

C R E A T I V E   J U I C E S F L O W

WOULD YOU LIKE A GLASS?

OR A PITCHER?   Or an oasis?

hey let go a her!
Pleeez I beg you for God sake...
nooo heyyy.
!

words & Pictures.
A single word makes a thousand pictures.

A picture makes a thousand words.

You will see the good and bad sides of a single word.

The ladder takes you to the part everyone wants.

For getting

forgetting

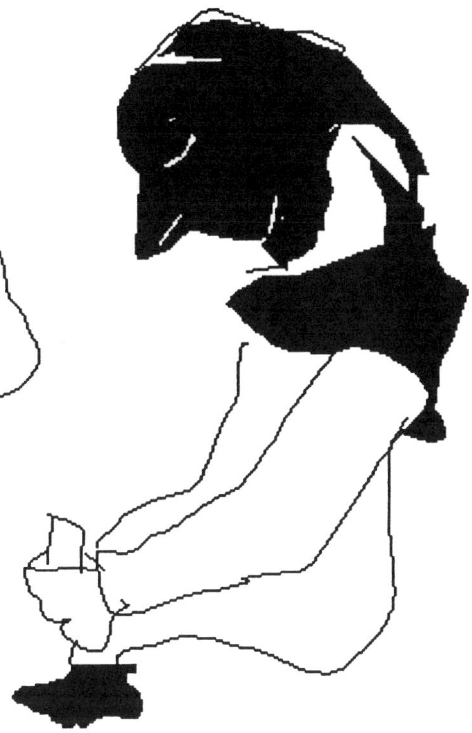

forgetting
for getting

Forget forget.
Peace arrives.
And you are still.
Bow your head
Let the memories run out.
Let the heart not chase toys.

famous

with fame we tattoo the smile

words & Pictures

FAMOUS
FAME MESS

With fame, the sleepless nights, planning the future
or fighting the present in silk pajamas.

To achieve recognition is
To gain incredible adoration,

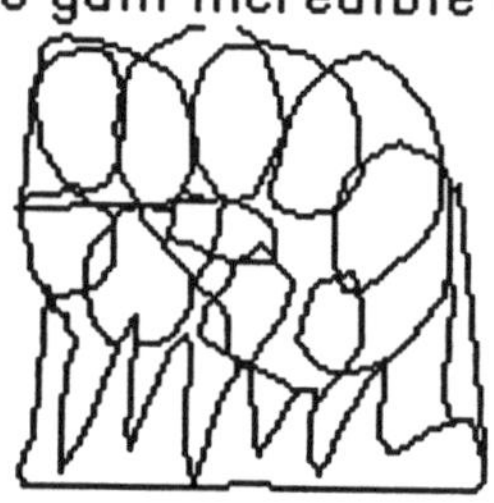

To be famous is
To be the CENTER
of the world

ANONYMOUS FAME: All the rewards without the punishment. The recognition of form without face. Financial gain in a private domain

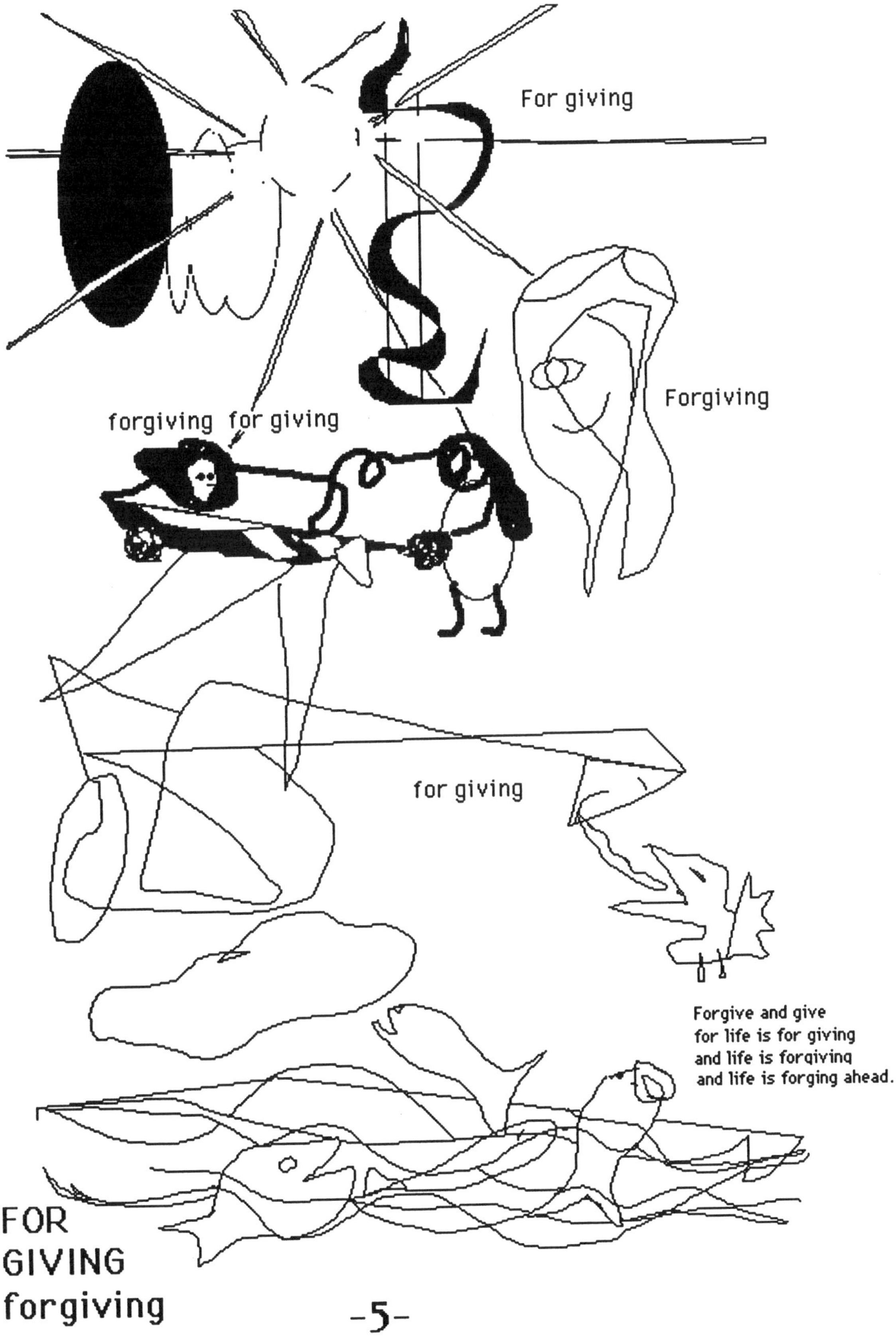
For giving
Forgiving
forgiving for giving
for giving
Forgive and give
for life is for giving
and life is forgiving
and life is forging ahead.
FOR
GIVING
forgiving

MOUTH

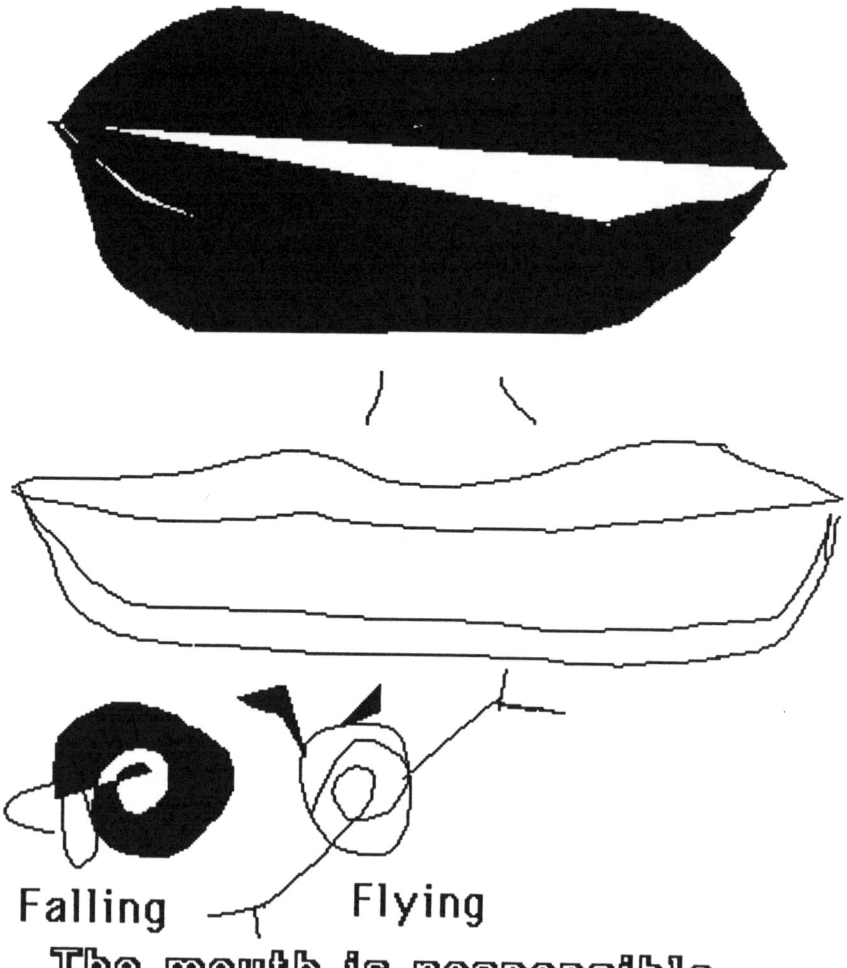

The mouth is responsible.

I love you-I loved him- I love steak- I'd love to I love that dress
I love little children - I love this - I love everyone - what is love?

Movement makes thoughts
light. Thoughts after movement
sets things right.
When movement is hard
laughter will do.
Or a good conversation with a
new point of view.
Do not sit still.

Moving is what God
intended for us. Two arms to
swing, two legs to stride,
a head to turn and thoughts
to exercise our will.
Do not sit still.

Move up, or down or
all around. you'll feel grounded.
Do not sit still.

Life is movement. Pick your
transportation. It's your key to
contentment.
Do not sit still.

GLADLY OASIS THREE

Fortunes & Bromides

Nothing prevents happiness but lack of a shiny word to remind you what you did, what you do, what you can do, who you were, who you are, and who you will always be

Get thee to an oasis. Your problems dissolve

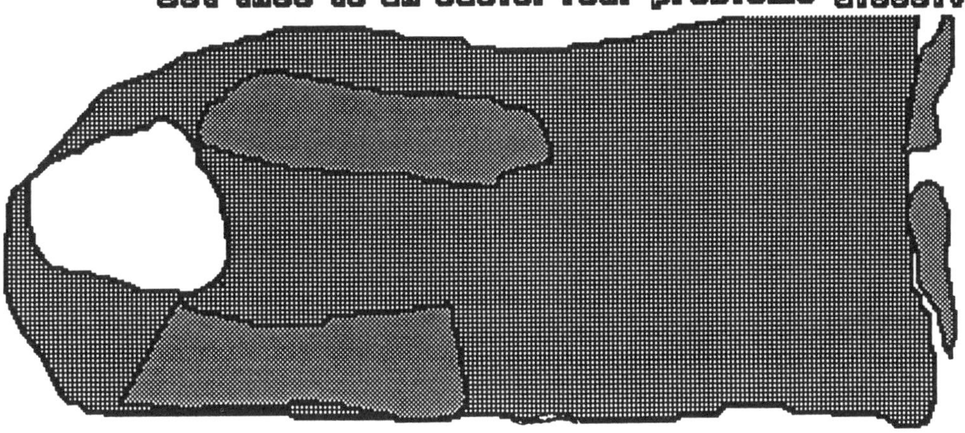

Ask **"TELL ME ABOUT..."** filling in the question or subject you want answered. Then choose one number or more from 1-106. Find the number(s) below for the fortune.

1 tYou need a friend's voice, not advice.
2 Seek and you shall find
3 Something unexpected.
4 The unexpected is what you need
5 Attach every value to friendship.
6 Persistence pays.
7 Pay the price. Make a move.
8 Stop a moment to be still.
9 A trip helps.
10 It's happening already.
11 Forces are working for you.
12 kindness pays.
13 find your center, lose your ego.
14 Your guess rules.
15 Find it in least expected place&time.
16 Really look, then stop.
17 Harmony results
18 ask any expert.
19 Take it in stride.
20 Wait two days and then act.
21 Strength is here.
22 Purpose is unknown.
23 Own your own thoughts.
24 Space for your actions
25 An unholy alliance doesn't work.
26 Single journey suffices to find out .
27 Now's the time to make solid resolutions.
28 Own yourself - no shares.
29 Find a way out of present situation.
30 Certain facts play with your life.
31 Train yourself
32 Figure out events
33 Step away
34 Spontaneous healing.
35 Read agendas in the eyes.
36 start it over again.
37 wear your smile inside out.
38 How much is it worth to you?
39 tedious journey.
40 A major future.
41 Check it through
42 Do it anyway
43 Go along for now
44 Repeat advice that worked.
45 Create spirits.
46 Thoughts have a new place.
47 You will improve your success.
48 Faith the issues.
49 compliments of the Great Chef in the sky.
50 go along for a while.
51 repeat advice that worked
52 create spirits
53 Thoughts have a new place
54 Faith the issues.
55 Believe the answers.
56 Discard the lies.
57 Faith is strong and attracts gold.
58 create spirits.
59 It ain't kosher if it's too hard.
60 Rely on the strongest person around---Yourself!
61 Correct the dots then connect them.
62 Close old door - open new one
63 Rewards corrupt decision.
64 Your magic moment.
65 Interrupt negatives w/ smile.
66 99.9% of your worry is fiction.
67 Stay in charge of emotions.
68 Your riddles solve themselves.
69 Spend time with higher thoughts.
70 Reflect on the day's unexpected events.
71 Talk to yourself in pleasant ways.
72 Gain insights by letting go.Wait before answering.
73 Wisdom follows.
74 Invisible systems below surface..
75 Invisible systems below surface.
76 Yesteryear manifests todays events.
77 Vast changes occur swiftly..
78 Promote yourself to high position
79 Stop using another's explanation.
80 Rid yourself of a cliche each day.
81 Judge not. It robs you of energy
82 Throw out labels of judgement.
83 Startling news awaits you each day.
84 Be aware of the minute (my-nute)
85 Forget to look i into mirror today.
86 Practice patience in answering.
87 Praise everything you see.
88 For now trust yourself
89 Owners don't exist.
90 Many time you fool yourself.
91 It's easy to love if you drop ego.
92 No payback. Do it for virtue.
93 Leave well enough better.
94 Sincerity counts.
95 Clutter works against you. Straighten it out.
96 Credit due you. Watch the mail
97 Freedom opens your heart.
98 Lend a hand and you'll have four.
99 Inspire yourself with breathing.
100 When you act, cease doubting.
101 When you doubt, cease actions.
102 The more you explain, the less you understand.
103 Get out before it's too late.
104 Spend a portion of time with good friends
105 Arm thyself with silence.
106 Screen what comes to mind before allowing it in.

TAKE ANOTHER LOOK

Fortunate is he who needs no fortune

A man with a temper has a live in enemy.

To have an **ADVANTAGE** don't **GET EVEN.**

In life one never comes out even. One is either ahead or behind.

The **big man** near the **mountain** (invisible)
The **mountain** near **the Earth** (not seen)
The **Earth** near the **galaxy** (a dot)
The **galaxy** in the **universe** (fits on a hangnail)
The **universe** (unfathomable)
The **big man**. Where is he now?
Somewhere in the universe.

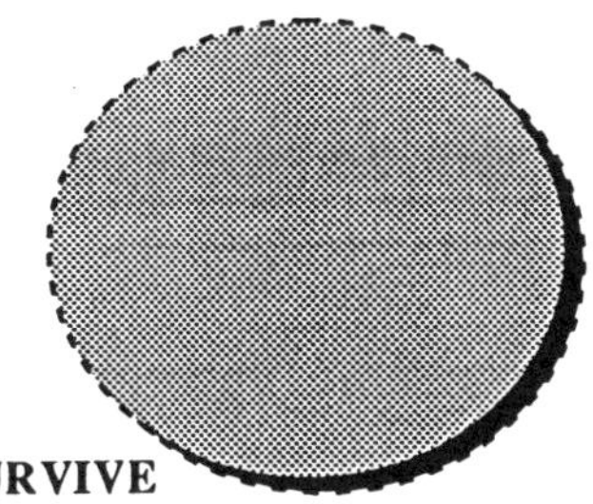

VALUE

I CANNOT CRITICIZE ANY VALUE THAT ALLOWS MAN TO SURVIVE

"The height of a man is not as relevant as the depth "

"Value is not to be reckoned with the same register as cost."

"Value comes over time. What is valued is nurtured without thoughts of recompense.

"Beauty that is an end in itself leads to ends that are not beautiful.

"He cannot read. He is not rich. He is ignorant in society's mind. Yet he is happy and has not hurt any man nor creature. He does not lust to covet another's ideas or property and finds joy in everything and everyone. When night comes he sleeps with an easy head. I would judge his values to be unsurpassed and his abilities of the highest. I learn from him each day.

"Dictated values are pasted onto the next generation. As soon as one is in hot water and gets unglued, these values fall away."

Thru The Years I've Noticed

1. An alibi will not fill the hole in the heart.
   Only truth is thick enough to do it.

2. When I stopped searching
   the answer gazed into my eyes.

3. Life is a swim in the sea
   amongst sharks and dolphins

4. Forget your own foolish wish.
   Allow God to pick the gift. for you.

5. Take care walking up the ladder of success . Those on the top rungs
   may lose their balance and fall on top of you.

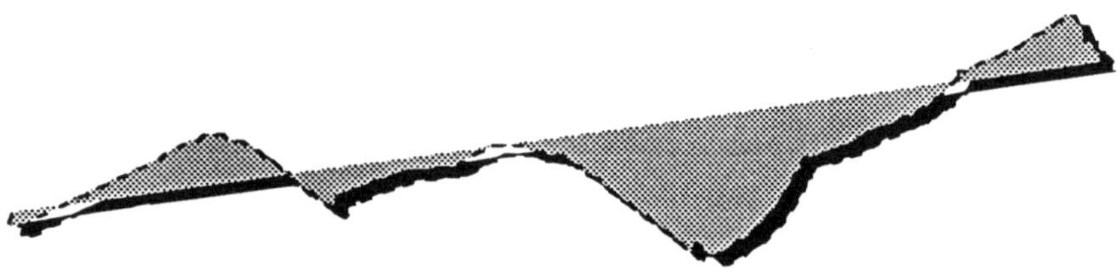

I t is our own thoughts that keep us balanced on the most perilous climbs.

6. **TIME**
Yesterday is unfaithful -
it's gone away
Tomorrow is a fickle beauty. -
it doesn't keep promises.
Today is the time that will work for you.
Give it your attention.

7. **WINDS OF FORTUNE**
The **East** wind blows a fortune to you today.
Tomorrow the **West** wind blows it away.
The **North** winds lets you forget
While the **South** wind banishes regret.
Let the winds blow as you bend with its flow.

Mixed together they provide the mosaic of your life. It is all very beautiful.

8. **WHILE YOU'RE HERE**
Don't forget to think kind words
Then you needn't plan to say them.
They will unfold as a refreshing breeze
Rising from beneath
To travel earth and sky.
And the breeze will always be with you.

Down to Earth, the same balance subdues the shock of potholes.

Real Fortunes I

Further delay helps

Reach a plateau soon

Pinpoint the next step

Rely on cool to your warm desire

Find a protected place and proceed.

Your frame of mind helps the picture

A yes is around the corner. Don't yield

There's a procedure that fits. Keep trying.

Novel approach fits present situation.

Family situation irons out or fades away.

Cozy evening coming your way.

The universe is a mirror

Experiment and see a new image.

Weather this storm calmly and it will be fine.

Whatever you do with tranquility works.

Unforeseen trip.

Serendipitous smiles.

Breakthrough - act quickly on the opportunity.

REAL FORTUNES II

(Begin with an unbiased observation of a situation)

Keep gathering data.
From your vantage point you see what's happening
Disappointments are not suitable input.
Stillness is also an action.
Whatever you think paints itself on your face.
Don't yield to pressures or promises
Only to what is right
Invent theories and formats to carry you forward.
Be free in your approach when solving riddles.
As soon as you change your thought pattern,
major problem is resolved.
Energy will bring freedom and friends.
Calmness is a buffer to difficult people at your
work place.
Make a plan, adjusting as you move along.
Don't force goals. It delays progress..
Don't allow sad illusions to make you (don't) **give in or**
(don't) **give up.**

THINGS TO NOTICE

Notice the things that are habit. For these are things you must change to rescue yourself from mediocrity.

Notice your reaction to those with different points of view. They point to treasure.

If you ride a horse backwards he'll soon outdistance you.

The hardest rock fears the softest water.

Without a tail to swish, man provides a feast for flies.

When you look into a mirror you cannot see ahead

Make do with little and you will love much.

No dog in his right mind would talk to a computer, nor a sane cat purr a fax.

Mock not your fellow man. He copies you.

A bad word spoken in jest darkens the light of the very best..

Dreams are the limbs of life. Hang in there. Use them.

A drop of water transforms to live forever.

All is not lost. Keep up your nerve and wait for the next beginning. Remember Life revolves.

Don't fret over trifles so that you may rejoice in ______ your heart **.LOVE.**

.Look long and carefully at offers made. Let questionable awards. pass.

<u>When your heart is ready your eyes will see. your hand will open. the. gift will come. Be at peace.</u>

MIRACLES

If there's a change in the weather, prepare for something better.

Unfolding is a question of private time and passionate thoughts

Every precious thought pays you dividends

Only humans proclaim their higher values while living by their baser instincts.

A train whistles its warning. A man whistles his fears. Don't challenge either.

Slowly proceed & you will see many wonders.

In opposing camps Saint and sinner are of the conviction: **<u>"Nothing"is Good"</u>**

Men stand superior to women when they give them their seat.

From a single word a life rearranges itself.

Finish what you begin. It is a virtue.

Apes have our eyes without our sham.

Any ointment will heal that is applied with a gentle heart. Sounds heal in the same way.

A stain cannot sustain the illusion of elegance.

Who steals from another's work steals from himself. He seals himself off from the muses and a stately peace of mind.

A slammed door does not win the argument.

23 fortunes to file.

1.TAKE YOUR MEDICINE AND MAKE THE LEAP

2.Bite your tongue and save the world.

21.Examine gems in your head to see if debris slipped in.

7.Silence can bear any burden.

3. Don't let a professional ventriloquist put words in your mouth.

16. Never never never NEVER say never (except in an emergency).

8.The highest mountain is your firmest ally.

9.Thought creates opportunity.

4.Hurry to your next good thought.

10. Behind each successful person stands a kind word.

14.Mission Accomplished. On to bigger things.

5. Paint a bold picture and don't let it go.

15.PLAN THE PAST & REMEMBER THE FUTURE.

6. Better than gold and mansions: energy and kindness.

11. Watch what you hear. The word eaten by the ear is digested by the heart.

23. A wonderful tomorrow begins today.

17. Keep your eyes innocent & you sleep sweet.

19. If you don't fit this puzzle perhaps you're in the wrong box.

13.Be a governor. Pardon yourself.

20. If life hands you a lemon make lemonade. If life gets you P.O'd make pisstachio.

18. You're the piece of the puzzle you're trying to solve. There's a better space that fits like a glove.

22. Everything you think, will occur this week.

12.YOU'RE ON TRACK. DON'T GO BACK.

WRITE YOUR OWN FORTUNES. BE VERY SPECIFIC TO YOUR NEEDS. SEE WHAT HAPPENS IN THE NEXT 2 WEEKS .

WORKING PHILOSOPHY

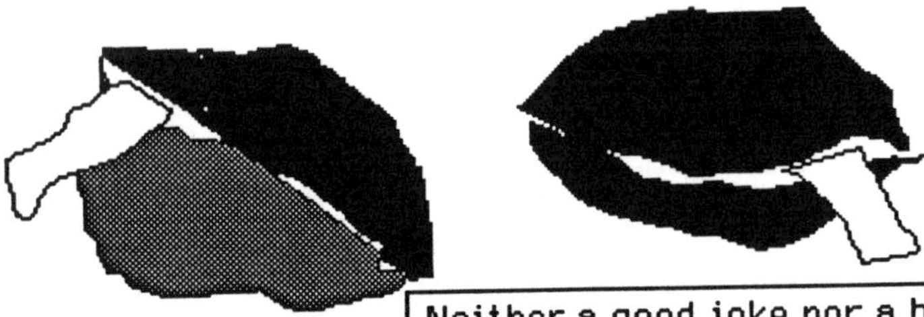

The riches you receive you richly deserve.

Neither a good joke nor a bad drunk is an excuse for unkind words.

Expect rocks when you dig for gold

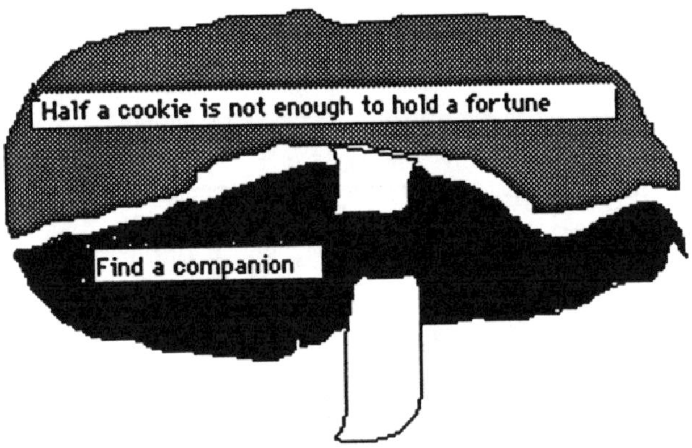

Another half makes you whole.
It looks for you
Meet it halfway.

Your fortune brings you in contact with the right person to understand your ideas.

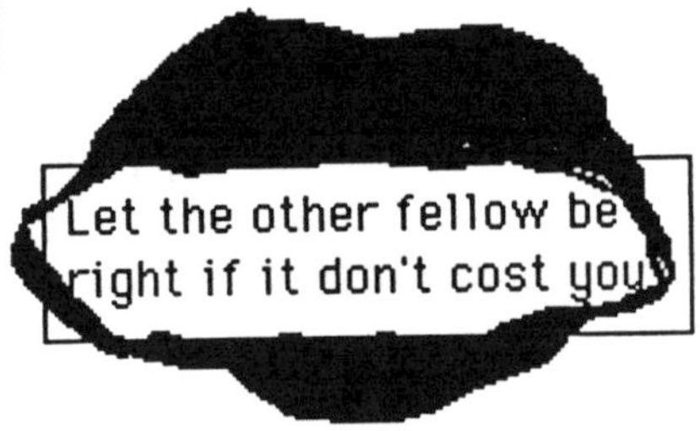

Let the other fellow be right if it don't cost you

Don't touch his heart yet. Shards of glass remain.

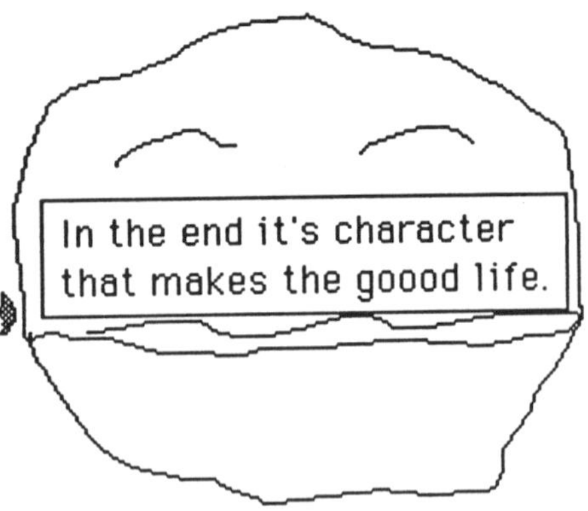

In the end it's character that makes the goood life.

HINDI FORTUNES

IN THE MANNER OF HINDI SENSIBILITY
DEEP ITS ROOTS. HIGH ITS BLOOM
FAR REACHING ITS RAYS
FED BY THE KIND RECEPTION OF EARTH.

1. Nothing is more valuable than a faithful friend. Nothing is as destructive as a faithless one. To encounter the one and be spared the other is the greatest blessing one can wish for.

2. We look at the same world and snap different pictures.

3. He who feels secure lures danger from its sleep.

4. It's morning and life waits.

5. It's evening and dreams begin.

6. Copy yourself when you're at your best.

7. **Engage yourself** only in proper behavior and thought. In time, behavior and thoughts become habits **you're married to** and **cannot divorce yourself from** easily.

8. Cleanse yourself daily, for dust travels far to ride upon your shoulders

THE SOUL OF ANOTHER

SEE IT- Sense what's invisible to human sight.
FEEL IT - A wisp of wing in rapid flight
HEAR IT - the comfort of angels sing through the night.
TOUCH IT - the awesome burning healing light.
TASTE IT- the bitter-sweet joy of living right.
The soul grows within us daily.
As we grow within it.
It is our recompense
For staying in the world that makes little sense.

oasis

9. Steady your mind so that no shout, look or circumstance can unhinge it.

10. Your resolve cannot compete with God's decree.

11. Look at the thoughts you wear. Sort them for cleaning, ironing out, throwing away or letting them be.

12. Don't defend what is indefensible.

13. Pray to do what you were meant to do, and to stop doing what is injurious to yourself or another.

14. **Wouldst thou be a good friend? Copy thy dog. Learn what he would teach you. Hold thy tongue when it would bark or whine. When you hear a friend at the door or see one in the street, jump upon him with alacrity and sweet sounding voice and wag thy tail endlessly so as to express thy complete and unconditional love.**

oasis

need help buddy?
hey let go a her!
Pleeez I beg you for God sake...
nooo heyyy.
!

The FORTUNES of ALPHABET I

ABCDEFGHIJKLMNOPQRSTUVWXYZ

To prevent your becoming too much of an adult prone to hardening of the Heart-aries let us go back to your childhood of Alphabet memories, where you sang your way through the A-B-C's feeling oh so proud of yourself. Here the fortunes will do the same.

the alphabet of
FORTUNES

(Accidental meetings become mergers)

As holes appear, fill 'em up, or jump over them.

Believe what helps. (Brains are vastly over rated)

Crossroads - If you've been here before - and turned back
Now's the time to cross it with élan. (Don't COMPARE bridges.
CROSS them all.)

DECIDE! Yes **DECIDE!**
As you move along. (Depend on a strong person - <u>Yourself</u>

(Energy is the basic unit of good luck)

Eureka! Solution comes without struggle.

the alphabet of
FORTUNES

Fast! Do things fast today! Outrun your thoughts!
(The farther you go the easier life becomes.)

Give it up!

(Grin and share it.
If you bare it now,
you won't have to
bear it later.)

Have your way. Be HAPPY!

Happiness is partly getting - partly giving - and partly neither.

('Ignorant' is an insult to the ignorant and a challenge to the the wise.)

It's the "I" that will not see the things more important than the "me"

Just be loving - Let the judges hang themselves. You're already acquitted. (Judges have a hard time disrobing.)

the alphabet of
FORTUNES

ALPHABET FORTUNES P.3

(Knowledge is sharp. Use carefully as a knife in a dark kitchen.)

Kiss it off! Twas said by one impressed with himself, imprisoned within himself.

Leap, don't jump.

Leap before it's too late.

Mercy! Have mercy!

Annoint thyself and those you meet with mercy.

(Mind over matter. Marvelous miracles.)

Noise – no noise – listen to the music from the sky.

(Nimble Escapes

When stuck there are 10 ways to proceed.

1. this way (North)
2. that way (South)
3. half way (East)
4. the other half (West)
5. go up
6. go down
7. go under
8. go over
9. go around
10 go nowhere

(Let the answer come to you.)

What was that? God pinching you.
Waking you from the comfort zone.
Now stretch way out.
OUCH!! Now what was *that?*
That's the new place you're growing to.

(OPEN
Anything shut
you can open
& vice-versa.
With a shut mouth, an
opportunity opens
& vice-versa.)

(Petty talks lead to Petty walks.
Walk away from the petty -
Your step enlarges)

Proceed. Payoffs ahead.

Quoth the Raven "Never More!"
Never think small.
More is behind the door.

(Question yourself, not others.
inherit your own wisdom.)

the alphabet of
FORTUNES

Rent your head to wise minds.

(Riddles hold the answers.
Answers hold the riddles.
Wise men riddle your answers
but never answer your riddles.)

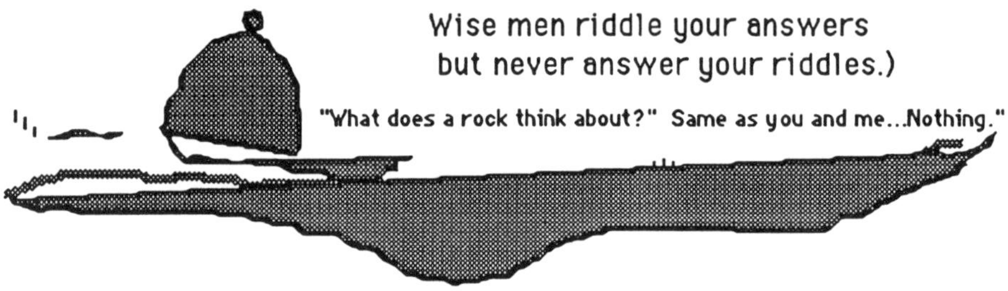

"What does a rock think about?" Same as you and me...Nothing."

Sorry – Use it more to others so it spreads around the world.

(Sincerity:90% silence 10% speech.
Insincerity: Turn the figures around)

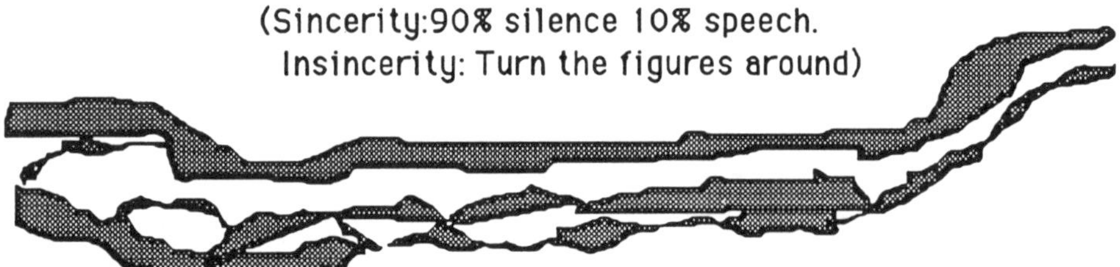

Toilet – Behind closed doors the real person comes out.

(TRAPS are painted gold.
What's beneath the alluring smiles
and smells? Dynamite.)

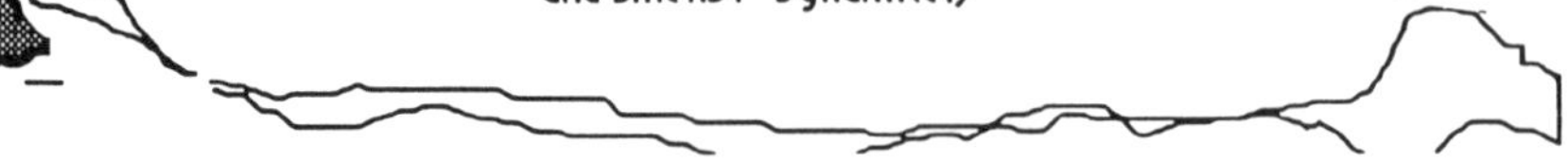

the alphabet of
FORTUNES

(Ulterior motives and interior reasoning culminate in exterior handshakes)

"why did they do that?"

nderstand your motives.
And you will understand theirs.

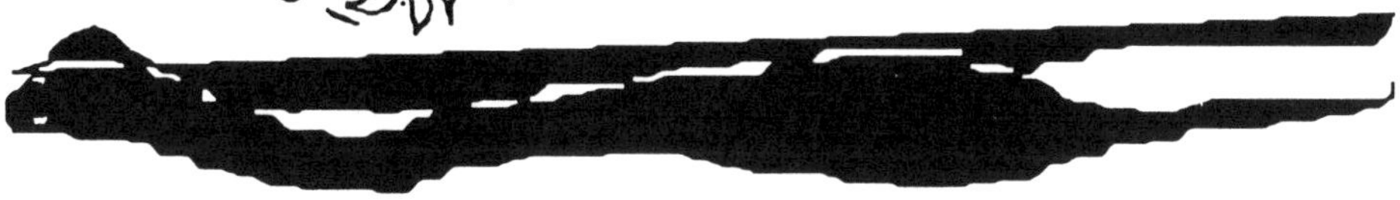

(Value visions. Yours & theirs)

ariety is the price of life.
Learn to enjoy each taste.

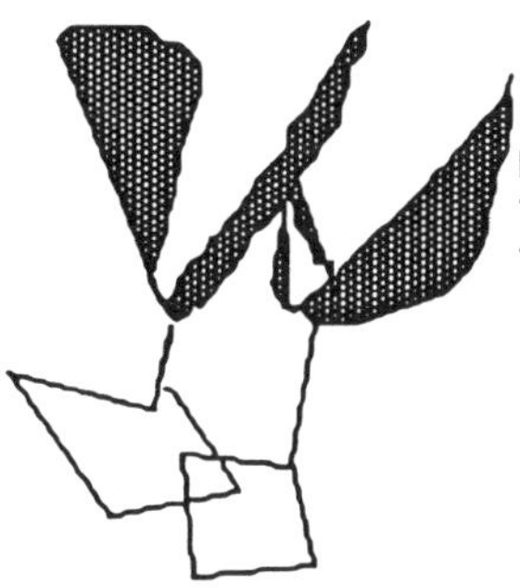

EIGH YOUR WORDS.
TOO HEAVY? LIGHTEN UP..
TOO LIGHT? GET SERIOUS.

(Weakness disappears. Energy returns simultaneously with a thougnt.)

the alphabet of
FORTUNES

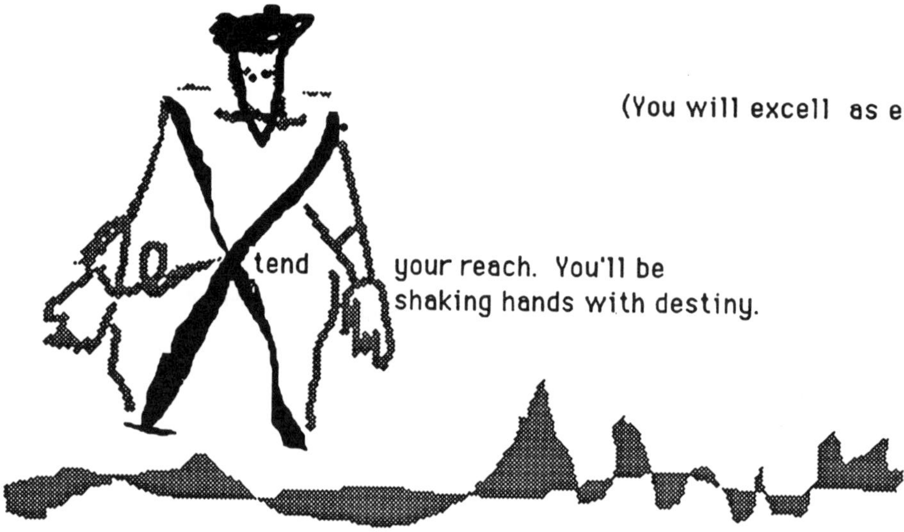

(You will excell as expected)

Xtend your reach. You'll be shaking hands with destiny.

Yesterday was fine. Use it as a ladder for today.

(You're helped along the path by strong hands. Don't doubt it.)

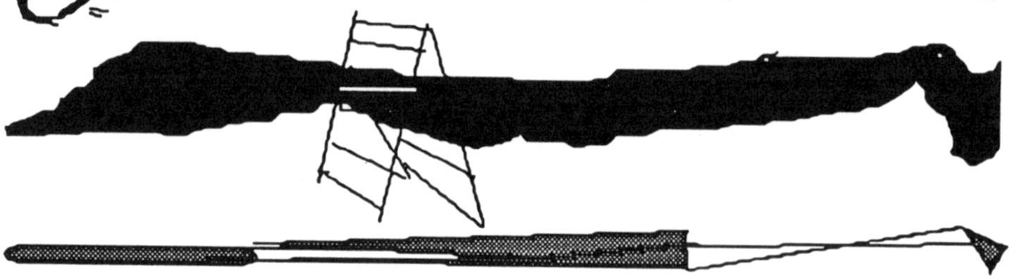

(The last letter rarely called up, but with noble bearing, is zealous, zestful, providing zeros for the millions you will make)

Zig Zag toward your earnest goal.

A B C D E F G H I J K L M N O P Q R S T U V W X Y Z

Here's another set of Fortunes alphabetically directed at you.

Enjoy them.

When you are thinking of a challenged area look randomly at one of the fortunes.
You might well discover the answer to your mood or thought.

Aa Bb Cc Dd Ee Ff Gg Hh Ii

Jj Kk Ll Mm Nn Oo Pp Qq Rr

Ss Tt Uu Vv Ww Xx Yy Zz

ALPHABET II

TWIN FORTUNES

(2 fortunes that express different views but are suited for one another.)

Enclose your dearest letters in this oasis.

THE ALPHABET OF FORTUNES (Twin thoughts)

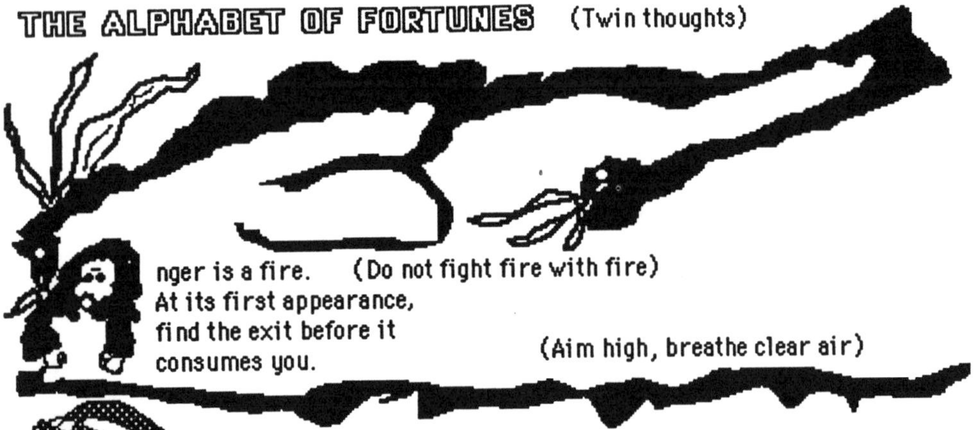

nger is a fire. (Do not fight fire with fire)
At its first appearance,
find the exit before it
consumes you. (Aim high, breathe clear air)

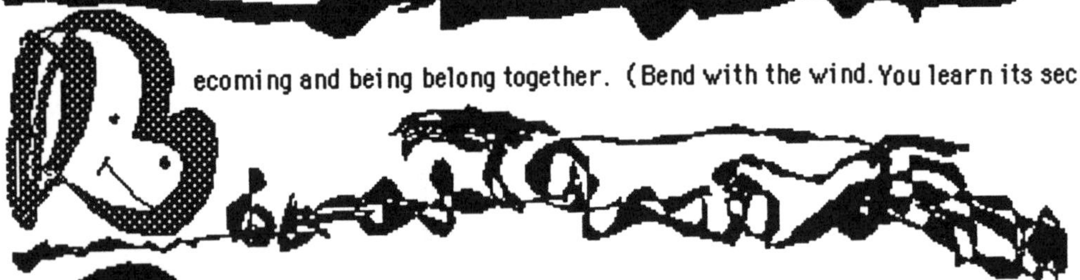

ecoming and being belong together. (Bend with the wind. You learn its secrets.)

limb your mountains and claim your rewards. (Chase after dreams and find a goldmine)

Critters crawl. Creatures climb. Creators codify.

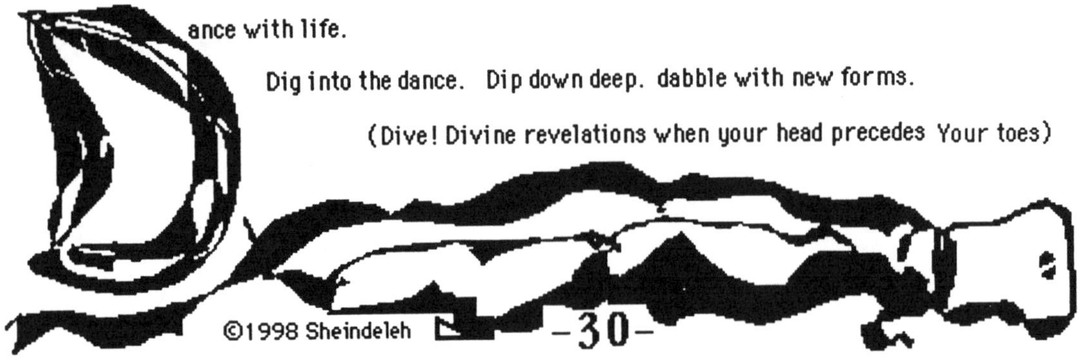

ance with life.

Dig into the dance. Dip down deep. dabble with new forms.

(Dive! Divine revelations when your head precedes Your toes)

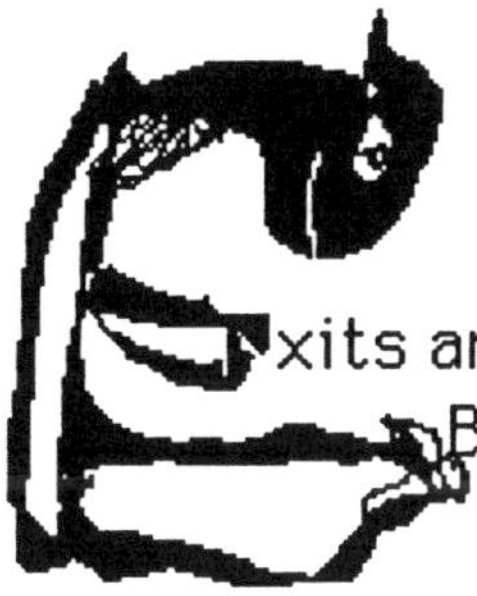

(Enormous energy needed to keep your eye on the fly -
Ignore the catcalls and applause till catch is made.)

Exits and entrances. One leads to the other.
Be prepared for the exchange.

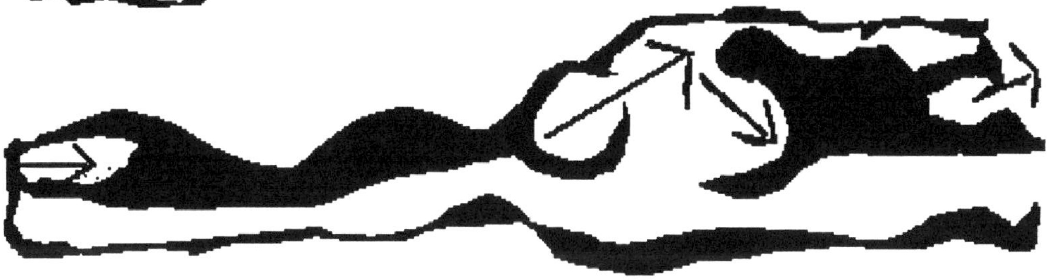

Freedom. Stop fighting. Stop fidgeting.
Forward with a smiling face and you
feel it down to your toes. (Faith alone fixes)

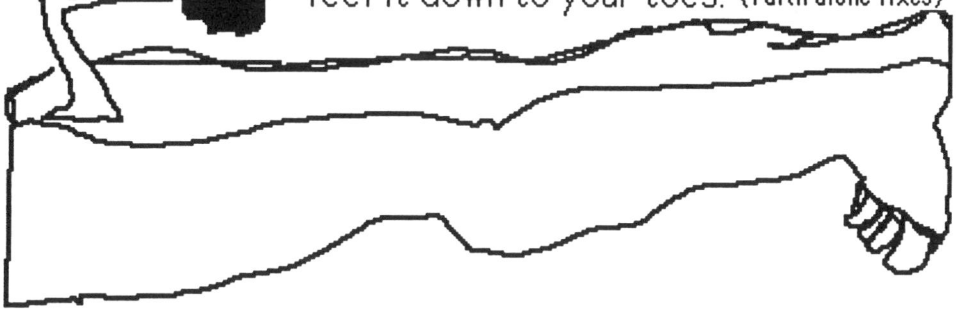

(Gratitude and graciousness without guile)

Gyrate your thoughts.
Past is not past. Present is a present.
Future rearranges furniture.
Gather and greet whoever, whatever, you meet. You gain
admission to golden opportunity.

Hang in there at all times.
Heaven wasn't built in a day.

(haste makes waste and false promises)

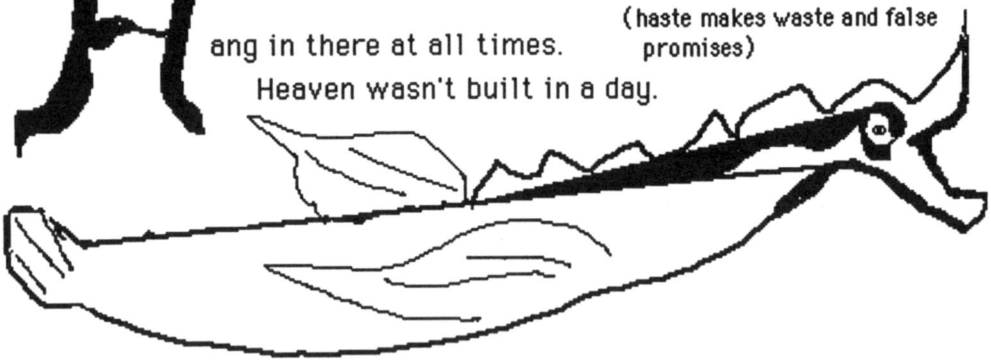

Imagine that!

Imagine what is good and it comes instantly.
In your mind, in your sight, in your sense, in your heart.and into your life.
Image not what is hurtful. It is illusion and will pass.

(If... if what? Change if to Step 1 I'll...
Change I'll to Step 2 Instantly I'll ...
Change Instantly I'll to Step 3 It's done...
With each done, take another step,
a million steps.
Start now with If... If what?)

(Be not judge nor jury nor joiner
and you enjoy the fruits of the universe.)

Jump! Up to clear thinking.
Left and right to see other options
NW, SE, and points in between to realize opportunities galore are yours for the taking.

Keep still when magpies chatter. (Kindness is its own reward)

Lead yourself Locate your self.
Like yourself. Liberate yourself.
Learn yourself. Listen to yourself.

(Leave well enough alone and concentrate on loving well enough together.)

Maybe this maybe that. T'aint bad sometimes to relax and maybe away a day. It's kinda' easy on the mind. Maybe...

(Make up your mind or your mind makes you up)

Needs are fulfilled. (Name yourself daily)

(Opportunity is the result of imagination pre-selecting manifestation)

Opinions and onions have a lot in common.
They cause the emotions to flow for no reason.
and often alienate others when indulged in without surcease by the users.

Private talks with yourself supercede any talks with experts. (Patience, poise, and puns get you out out of bad situation)

Question! Anything you're sure of.
Time to get out of a comfortable
ignorance.
(Quick action will save the day)

Resist running from situation.
Reach some simple decision and
act upon that tranquilly.
(Raise your hopes, it's going to be fine.)

Sail on sand, swim in soup
do silly stunts and then re-group.
Change your words, change your suit.
Sing silly songs and you'll recoup.

(Spin like a top
That's where you'll come out on.)

Take a vacation. take your time
ake a minute to make a rhyme.
Don't you hurry. don't you run
Take a while to just have fun.
In other words Take it easy...
You'll be glad you did after you do

(Time out. Put all those
chores, projects, and concerns
into the Tomorrow bin. And take
out your loving errands from the
Someday soon closet. Try them on.
See if they still fit.)

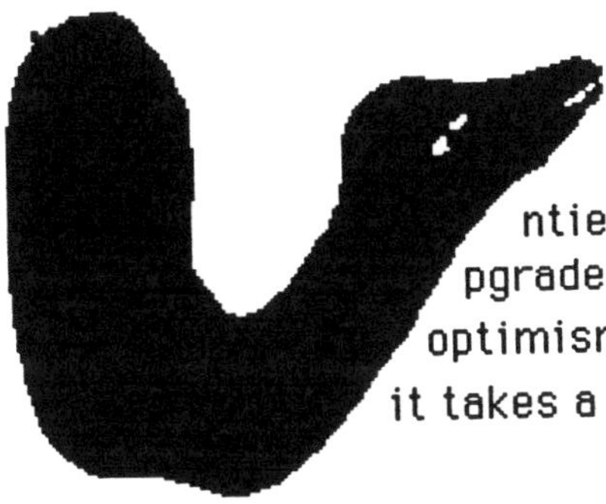

ntie those hands. Unite your mind. pgrade your smile. Use your God-given optimism to uplift your heart whenever it takes a spill. (Unusal things occur to change your usual way of thinking. All to the good.)

ictory comes to you through a series of events you follow through on.

(very is a word you will use for the next two weeks. "very good, very wierd, very sweet etc.")

here ever, whatever, who ever, whenever, whichever, why ever any situation puts you under stress wait for wisdom without a word. Clarity will appear when adrenalin dissapates. Head for the can. Sit on it and wait for wisdom.

Extend yourself this week to everyone you meet. Your world expands in equal proportion. You will be surprised how many covers you misread all these years including your own.

(Exceptions to the rule are the rule you should look into. What follows the rule is a slavish outlook to authority.)

Yes on the job is demanded .
Yes from acquaintances is shallow.
Yes between equals is exhilerating.
Your yes is always sincere. You gain from this gifting.

(Yield today to any demands or requests. Tomorrow the yield sign turns in your direction.)

Zones of comfort must be upgraded. They put zip into your life.

(Zip your lip. Don't let emotions slip. A little tip to keep your grip. Everything will feel better in a couple of hours)

DOTS LIFE

LOOK AT THE DOT . Dot's you in the universe

Look at this dot • Dot's you in the world.

Look at the next dot. o Dot's you in the neighborhood.

Now look at that dot. ● Dot is you looking in the mirror.

And look at this DOT.

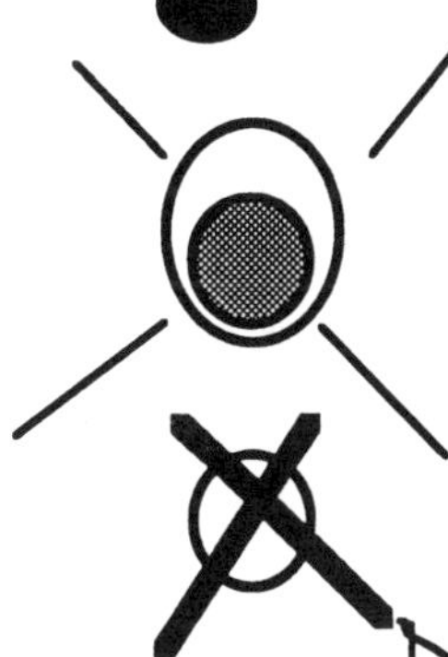

Dot's you with God

NOW FORGET THE DOT... **<u>AND FOLLOW LIFE'S FLOW...</u>**

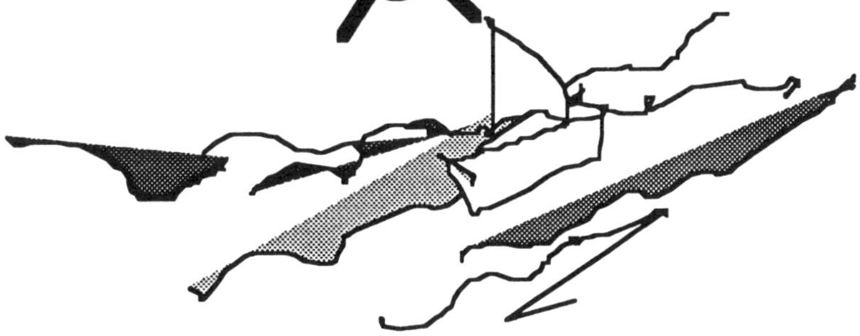

It's not only birds who 'sing by days'
and 'fly by nights'.

It seems..

A lion who moos
A cow who roars
A dog who purrs
A cat running with a bone
Put into human terms
All rush to believe it.

Each has his agenda baptized as the truth

When a man puts a foot in his mouth
He bites off more than he can chew

A man's place is where ever he can put his feet up.

A woman's place is where ever she puts her foot down

Talent is mined by the owner who digs for it

Money is a lazy way to avoid truth.
More folk move forward talking backward.
And vice versa.

Love's Fortunes*

Here's your wand. You get however many wishes you want if you can say them in a minute. It's fun.

You are the love dictator. Anything you say comes to pass.

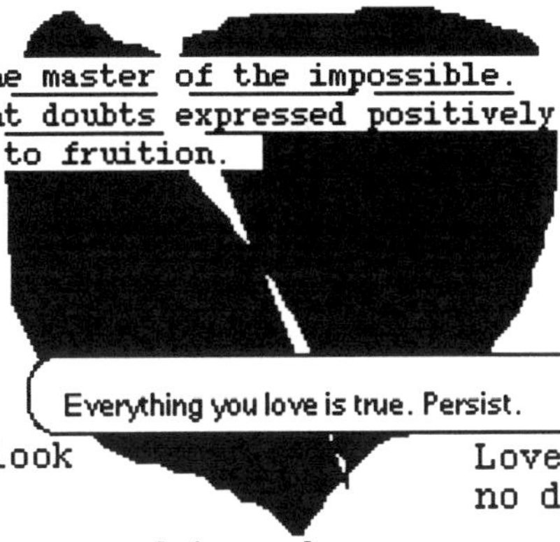

You are the master of the impossible. All present doubts expressed positively will come to fruition.

Yes it's there in your own back yard. Why do you look far afield?

Everything you love is true. Persist.

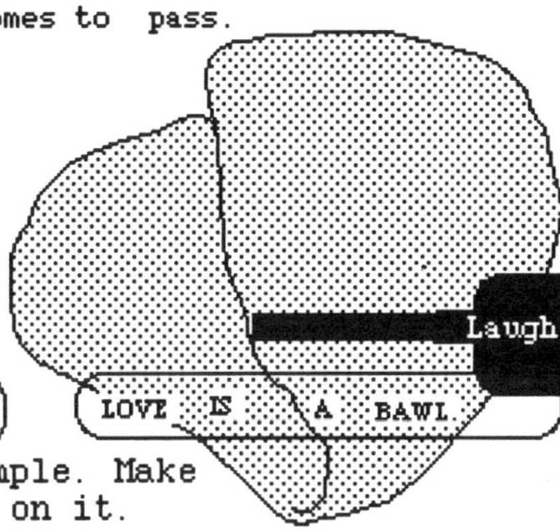

Laugh at it all.

LOVE IS A BAWL.

Love is simple. Make no demands on it.

You are in charge of joy. Anything you make up will happen to you.

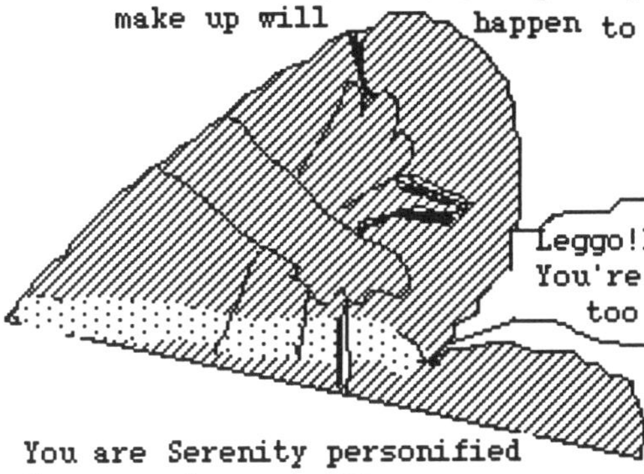

Leggo! Leggo Love! You're holding on too tight.

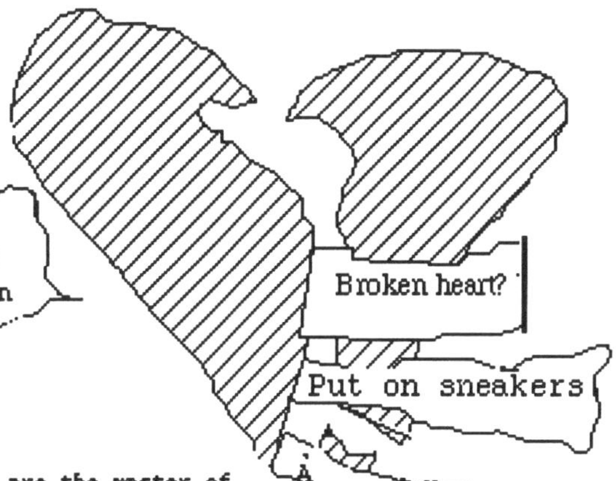

Broken heart?

Put on sneakers

Another game is about to begin

You are Serenity personified Every word you say shows composure.

You are the master of learning. You can learn from every person, place and situation.

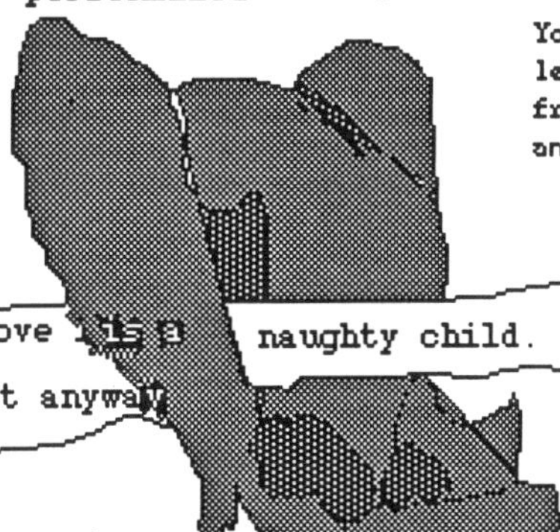

Love like fire is not product but process.

Love is a naughty child.

Embrace it anyway.

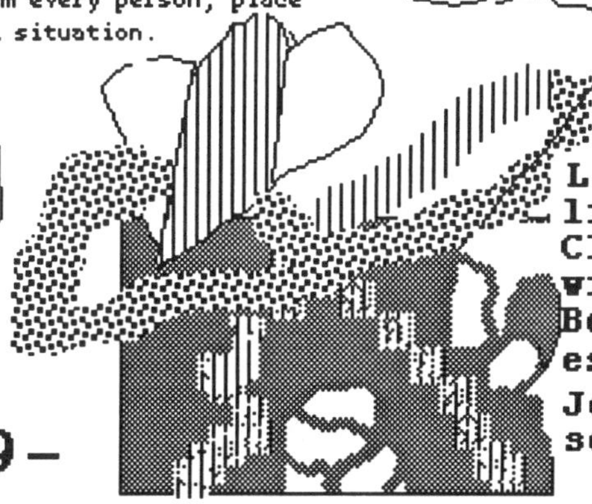

BALANCE

Love with like.
Closeness with distance
Bonds with escape.
Joy with sorrow.

THE CALMER THE LOVE
THE SWEETER THE LIFE.

LOVE I

Here today.
Gone tomorrow.

LOVE II

Gone today.
Here tomorrow.

True Love? look beyond fashion.

Love gift arrives. Looks good
What's inside? One never knows.

Express those love feelings that let you linger in everyone's soul.

TIMELY ADVICE...

WHAT IS TIME?
IT IS ENERGY AND ACTIONS.

WANTING THINGS UNDULY
RESULTS IN LOSING BOTH.

THE WISE HEART WILL
HAVE ALL IT DESIRES

THOSE WHO INSIST UPON THEIR WAY
SOON LOSE THEIR BEARINGS.

CALM THOUGHT IS A COMPASS THAT
LEADS SAFELY TO HIGHER GROUND.

TREATS OF THE SOUL CAN BE FOUND
EVERYWHERE YOU ARE.
DON'T OVERLOOK THEM IN MODEST
ENTERPRISES.

The more you can cope,
the more you'll have to.
Plan the leap.

CERTAINTY IS A BRIEF
NECESSITY. SOONER OR
LATER YOU WILL FEEL
THE NUDGE OF CONFUSION
THAT SAYS IT'S TIME TO
MOVE ON TO A HIGHER
VIEW WHERE THE AIR IS
THINNER AND THE THOUGHTS
ARE CLEARER.

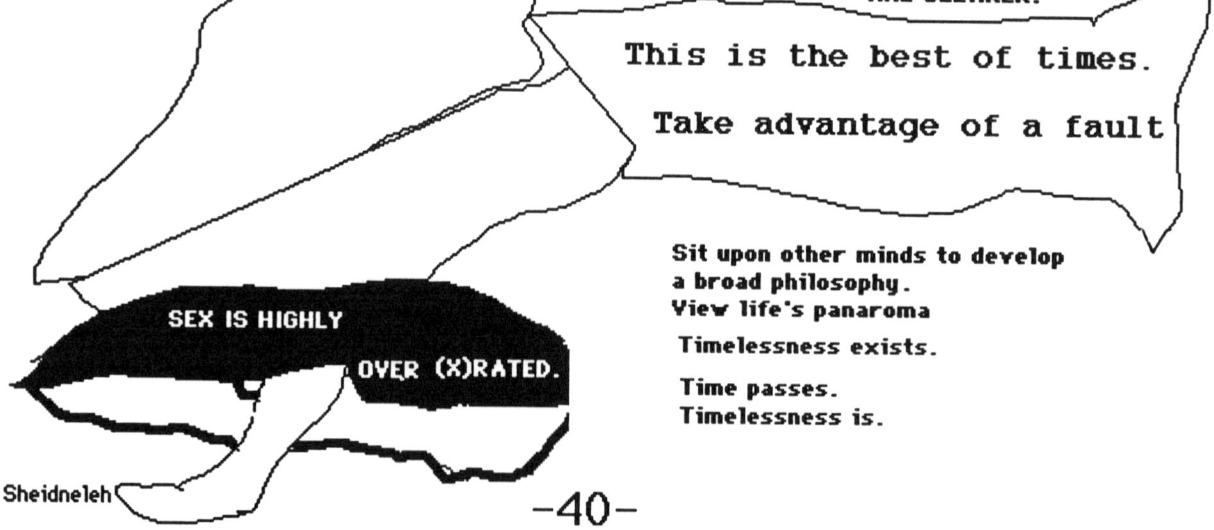

Sit upon other minds to develop
a broad philosophy.
View life's panaroma

Timelessness exists.

Time passes.
Timelessness is.

BE!HAPPY

BE!Happy Get a jeep. Blow your own horn.

BE!Happy Pass a hug on.

BE!Happy Give everyone a peace of your mind.

BE!Happy Your good actions pay off.

BE!Happy Your temperature rises,Your dreams unfold

BE!Happy Write a song walking along.

BE!Happy Let the world sing your songs.

BE!Happy You own what you appreciate.

BE!Happy Your eyes dance with another's

BE!Happy Identify with the best.

BE!Happy Find a friend in need.Share your journey.

BE!Happy Looking, you find true love.

BE!Happy The philosophy of a word will do it.

BE!Happy Precious moments increase.

BE!Happy Good intentions bring a windfall soon.

BE!Happy Rotate your thoughts.

BE!Happy Never you mind why you can't.

BE!Happy Quickly warm it up. Share with guests.

BE!Happy Treasures appear.

BE!Happy What you require is nestled within you.

BE!Happy Take the moment You're transfigured.

BE!Happy You're in charge of operations.

BE!Happy Believe that good surrounds you.It appears.

BE!Happy **Run around is over.**

BE!Happy -Your vibrations bringing personal gift.

BE!Happy Throw out doubts. Your ability sees you thru.

BE!Happy With a passion you win a long awaited award.

BE!Happy Face it all. You get what seems impossible.

BE! Happy Don't **manufacture** worry. It aint **selling.**

BE! Happy After the storm,the rainbow.

BE!Happy Your ship comes in quietly . Be ready for it.

BE! Happy Your independence grows in next 2 days.

BE!Happy Shorten expectations increase acceptances. Rewards.

BE!Happy Treat yourself to a new idea.You'll have a good laugh

BE!Happy Your success is reflected in accepting subtle gifts.

BE!Happy Ask no questions- tell no lies - Spread your joys.

BE!Happy The tiny joys contemplated can't be bought.

BE!Happy Treat yourself to a pat on the back.

BE!Happy The world owes you thanks.

BE!Happy Call a friend. You won't be sorry.

BE!Happy Take a bold and beautiful action NOW.

BE!Happy It is your destiny.

BE!Happy- You are blessed with courage & survival.

RHYME WITH REASON TO BASIC LIFE QUESTIONS

1. Stuck?

Stop all thinking let actions enter
Go from crowded mind to happy center.

2. Dissatisfied?

Don't pout.
Get right out.

3. Bored?

Widen the base.
Choose another space.
Don't fake it's true
Do something to make it true.
Look up at your goal

5. Face one thing at a time.

A major task to be done?
Treat it with fun,
Look at the whole
Then take any part
Forget the rest
Make a fresh start
Keep your focus.
Hocus Pocus
Now you're done
Wasn't that a lot of fun?
Now onto part 2
Forget any losses
Don't think about pleasing bosses
Just go at your project one thing at a time
You don't have to struggle
And you ***will*** make the climb.

6. Aargh!

What is a miracle happens this week.
As you once more begin on a long lucky
lightening up streak.

7. Want to be rich?

You're in the midst of worldly treasure
Yours to choose at your leisure.

8. Get Lucky

Make simple equations
To blend wishes with obligations
You will fulfill both.

9. Overdue

What is overdue
is on its way with interest to you.
(Could it be the tax?)
Hang in and relax

10. Scared Worried and Perplexed

You're working your mind too hard
Stop to have a chat with God
Then out for the day or bed for the night,
Throw a kiss to the world
And look toward the light
And know that everything
will turn out just right.
(Hasn't it always?)

11. SOMEONE TREATING YOU BADLY?

Whatever they do
It can't really hurt you
If you don't engage in their battle
Look up at your goal
Look into your soul
And let them box with your shadow.

12. LOSING YOUR HAIR

Remember Yul Bryner?
He was a real winner
And believe me, you are the same
Rely on your inner
And keep up your chinner
It's only another life game.

13. BEING SMART

We're all born with a brain
It's a matter of boarding the right train
Look deeply into anything
And your thoughts start whispering.

14. LOOKS

you think you're not good looking
It won't be perjury
To do your own plastic surgery
Before you go on any more trips
Put a smile on them thaar lips
Aaaah That's so much better.
You look magnificent.
(What rhymes with magnificent?)

15. INSULTS

High silence or 'Thank you my dear'
The arrow thus deflected
won't pierce your armor with its fear.

RHYME WITH REASON
TO BASIC LIFE QUESTIONS p.2

15. FINDING LOVE

You see it over here.
You see it over there
Always two by two
With not one left for you
If you've looked and never found it
Then here's what you must do
You must go about your business
And love will then find you
Chance meetings are the best.
If you go about your business
God will do the rest

16. MONEY WOES

If you'll keep on your toes
You'll find that money comes and goes
Only worries stay long after
So quit frowning. Produce laughter
And before you can say "Woe to poor me"
Your money will drift back from the sea

17. LOST OR STOLEN OR MISPLACED

STOP LOOKING STOP LOOKING
It's hiding you see
You were smothering it
and it longed to be free.
Go on with your life,
No backward glance
It will come back to you
by miraculous chance.

18. RELATIONSHIPS

Be true to yourself
and let go what must go
Twisting yourself like a pretzel
Hampers the flow.
You can do better
if your energy's free
Take some deep breaths
and laugh on high C.
(read three times) Ha Ha Ha
(then break into free laughter)

19. MOVING

Pack the boxes and stay carefree
Everything will turn out as it should be.

20. HEALTH

God works your heart
Your heart works your brain
Your brain works the guts
And it starts all over again.
So if healthy or even if sick
You can maintain or get back health
if you follow this trick.

Stop thinking, don't let your mind dwell
On ANYTHING, and you're sure to stay well.
you heard what I say.
You keep dwelling on things
and your brain rubs away.

Now your brain has imported
work to do for you.
And if you're always on the "wireless"
How can God get through to you. hah?
How can he? Can he? Can he? Can't!
He can't. Get off thinking and you'll see.
He'll be there immediately.

So if you want to be healthy don't overthink
Eat right, do right, You'll be alright.
You won't need a shrink.
Good night and have a happy
GESUNDTHEIT.

21. IN LOVE

Love is filled with grace for all
Without grace, love will fall.

22. CONTRADICTION

Is either growth or lip service
Both can make one nervous
The former is like an old suit outgrown
One must buy another to wear.
The latter is a belief on short term loan.
Wearing untrue words to appear fair.

23. PROCRASTINATION

To arrive at your destination
Let there be no hesitation
Don't put it off a minute
Or you won't ever begin it.

24. FRUSTRATION

is something you should mollify
Stop a moment, heave a sigh
Let your head clear and you will see
The frustration end easily.
Make a decision to go or stay.
To come to the problem a different way.
Or even on another day.
Be at rest and know
Problems come visiting
and then they really must go.

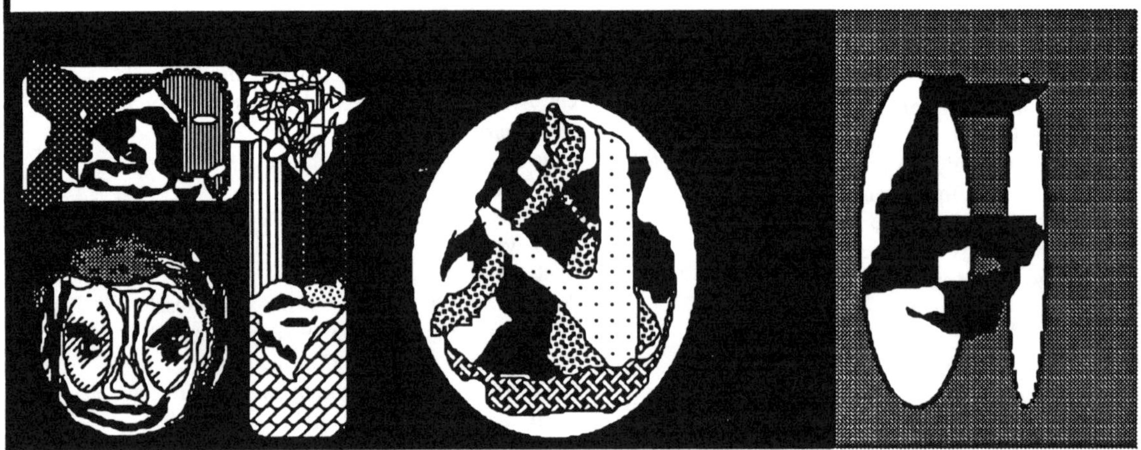

When cares are over or cares are few, you'll thank God for caring for you.

Quench not your aspirations to reach a higher state from a deeper inward journey. Paradox of reaching deeper to go higher.
Opposite each sad thought is a high one. Reach for it and the other will fall away.

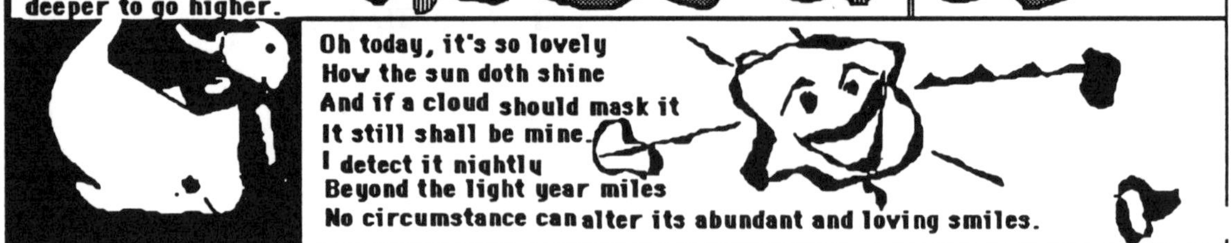
Oh today, it's so lovely
How the sun doth shine
And if a cloud should mask it
It still shall be mine.
I detect it nightly
Beyond the light year miles
No circumstance can alter its abundant and loving smiles.

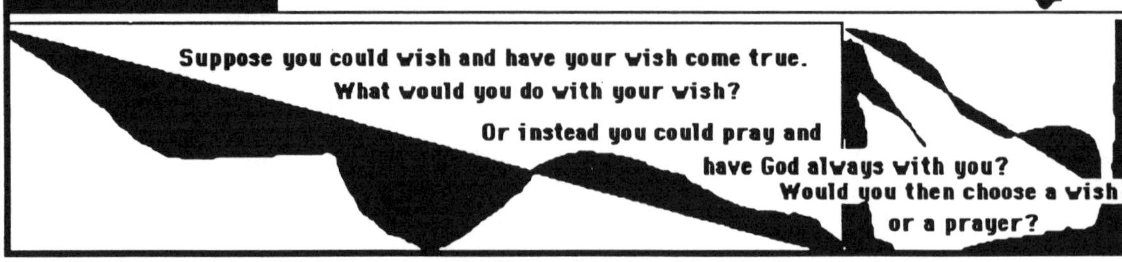
Suppose you could wish and have your wish come true.
What would you do with your wish?
Or instead you could pray and
have God always with you?
Would you then choose a wish
or a prayer?

Personal Touch, View, Feelings, Thoughts.

You can read books or read eyes or read the future or read intentions or read another's heart or read the skies or read the silences or read the palm or read the mind or read the past or read the mysteries of earth. Ah, to read you must cultivate the spirit and not mix it with the programs that are given you.

I see so much when there is so little and so little when there is so much.

We all speak in a fog of Ego.

Clarify yourself with pure water Free out the modems of ancient process. Let the air speak to you without your interrupting.

Re-runs of words, re-runs of anger. Memory has its false. All media traps the innocent in hypnosis of despair and excitement and innocuous promise. Let go of entertainment, entrainment, and you will rise first to the surface of life and then be joined by others swimming with their head above water rowing toward the gallant shores of serendipitous reality. Sacrifice your pettiness to enter wholiness, your ego to gain heroism, your pomposity to recoup your innocence. With clear eyes you know what to do with life's gifts.

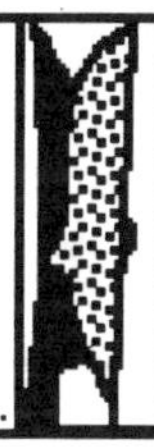

Time passes quickly, too quickly with desires. Without desire joy appears as a butterfly does without warning without promises and a moment lasts without past, present or future. The timeless lasts and the mind joins the moment neither going back or forwards bobbing up and down with the wave of eternity. The traces of the moment reverberate and there is no bitter aftertaste. We cannot push it or entreat it. All we need do is clear a space and hang out a welcome sign.

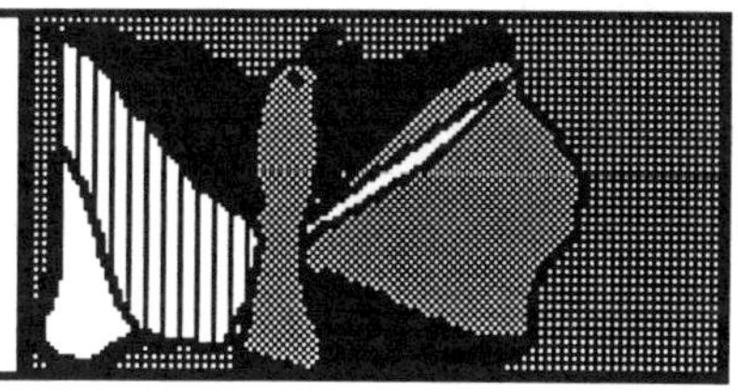

We are the dwarf to the universe which cares not about our "success" "our toys" "our struggles". It doesn't brag about its size, its longevity (not ever having taken a vitamin). You hear not a whimper when a star explodes or a meteor self-destructs. No litigation, no condemnation. Endless.

Correct me if I'm wrong but didn't we meet a lifetime or two ago and don't we have something still unsettled between us? I believe you still hold me responsible for something which I have truly forgotten. Let us regress to that spot some hundred years ago and see if we can come to some mutual understanding so that we may be friends in this lifetime.

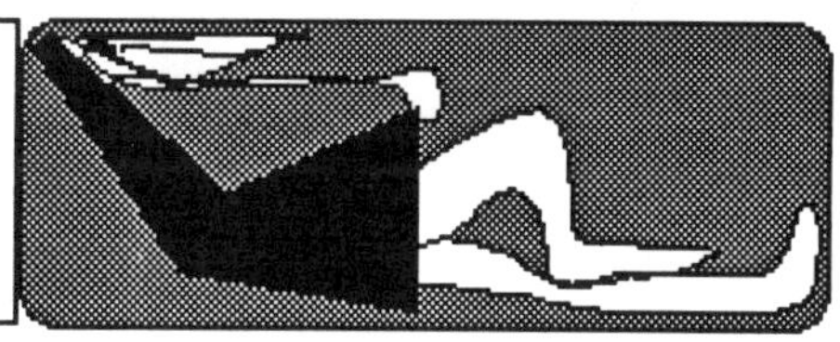

The words to indicate sight prevail in this land. And the blind must adjust to using them as well. But they are overworked and I'd like to see the other senses used. I'd like to feel the other senses used. I'd like to hear what she has to say. I'd like to taste the ocean. Do you sense what I'm getting at. I heard from her the other day and she touched me. Talk to you later. Do you get what I mean? Insights.

Beyond your nose lies a universe

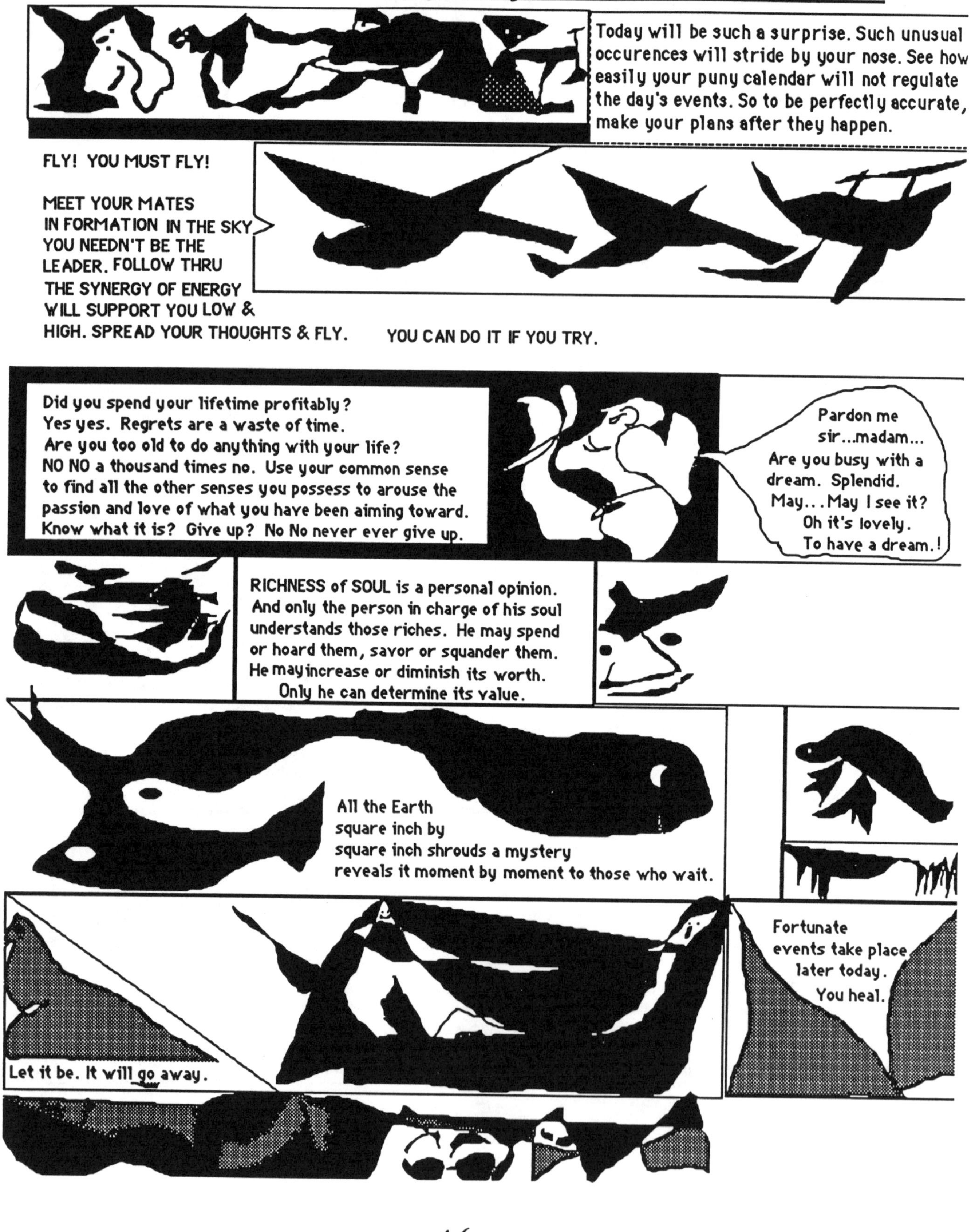

4 Find the question to the answer.

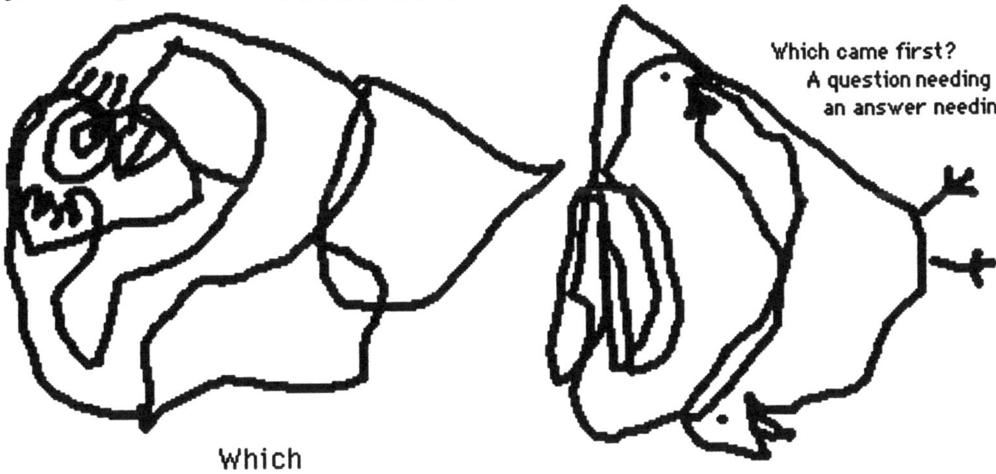

Which came first?
A question needing an answer or
an answer needing a question?

Which
came
first? the chicken or the egg?

OR THE ROOSTER?

or was it a simultaneous creation
And only afterwards
was the egg fitted inside the chicken
and the rooster placed strategically
Upon the chicken to fertilize the egg.

NEW QUESTION...

Which came second?
The chicken or the rooster?

YOU SEE EVERYTHING. YOU KNOW EVERYTHING. YOU HAVE EVERYTHING. TOUCH EVERYTHING. LOVE EVERYTHING. FORGIVE EVERYTHING. EVERYTHING IS HERE ALWAYS. EVERYTHING CAN BE SHARED. EVERYTHING IS EVERYTHING IS EVERYTHING. EVERYTHING IS BORN. EVERYTHING LIVES EVERYTHING DIES. EVERYTHING IS BORN AGAIN. EVERYTHING IS BEAUTIFUL. EVERYTHING DECEIVES. EVERYTHING GIVES PLEASURE. EVERYTHING GIVES PAIN. JOY IS EVERYTHING. LOVE IS EVERYTHING. HONESTY IS EVERYTHING. NOTHING IS EVERYTHING. SOMETHING IS EVERYTHING. YOU HOLD EVERYTHING

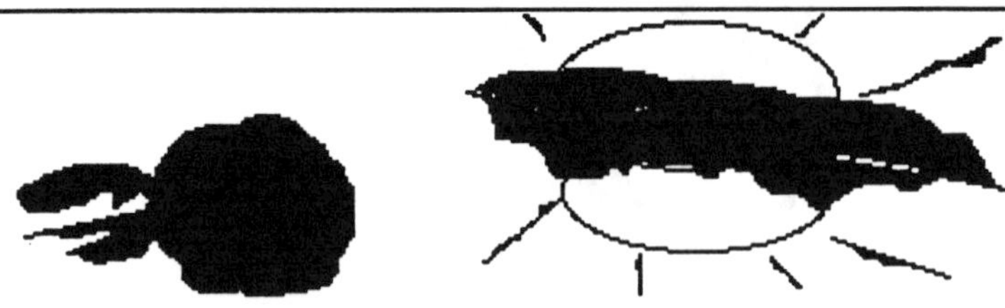

ACT NOW.
ACT SINCERELY.
ACT IN CRISIS
ACT WELL.
ACT KINDLY.
ACT W/FEELING
ACT SIMPLY.

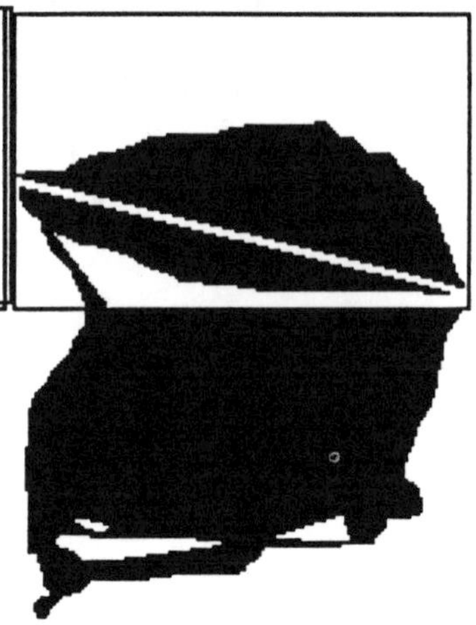

SELDOM WE SAY ALL WE WANT OR THINK AS DEEPLY AS WE CAN OR GIVE AS WELL AS WE OUGHT OR LAUGH AS MUCH AS SPIRIT DEMANDS OR FEEL AS FULFILLED AS WE WOULD LIKE OR HAVE SINCERE FRIENDS WHEN WE NEED THEM. I THEREFORE PROPOSE WE STOP UNTIL THE WORLD STOPS SPINNING ROUND OUR HEAD AND GET CALM AND LET THE RIGHT THOUGHTS AND PEOPLE AND LAUGHTER CATCH UP WITH US AND GIVE US THEIR BENEFITS OF OUR DOUBTS. WHEN WE GET SIMPLE, LIFE GETS BETTER.

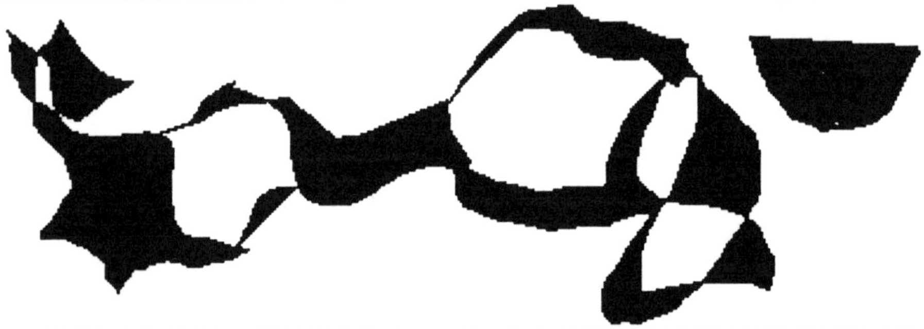

It is so easy to love not to choose it but to do it. So easy to breathe deeply instead of holding in anger. Easier still to listen, encourage with a smile what is said. To walk and talk with trees, grass, clouds, animals, spirits is illuminating. It isn't easy to run after the rewards of the world, and be steady in heart and mind for fear lies in all of this. It is necessary and easy to keep a promise. Share goodness and friendship. Less strenuous than judging or having pity. Find friends on your journey who are easy with everything.

Oh your heart sings like a buttercup's yellow.
And your ears hear like a Chopin étude.
And your smile unravels to speak to sweet strangers
and you know the words
to heal every wound

A peal of bright laughter
Smooths wrinkled tears
And the silence of love
Enfolds you to dream
Me happy Me happy. Momma you hear me.
Momma Me Happy. Me happy. Are you?
Me happy.

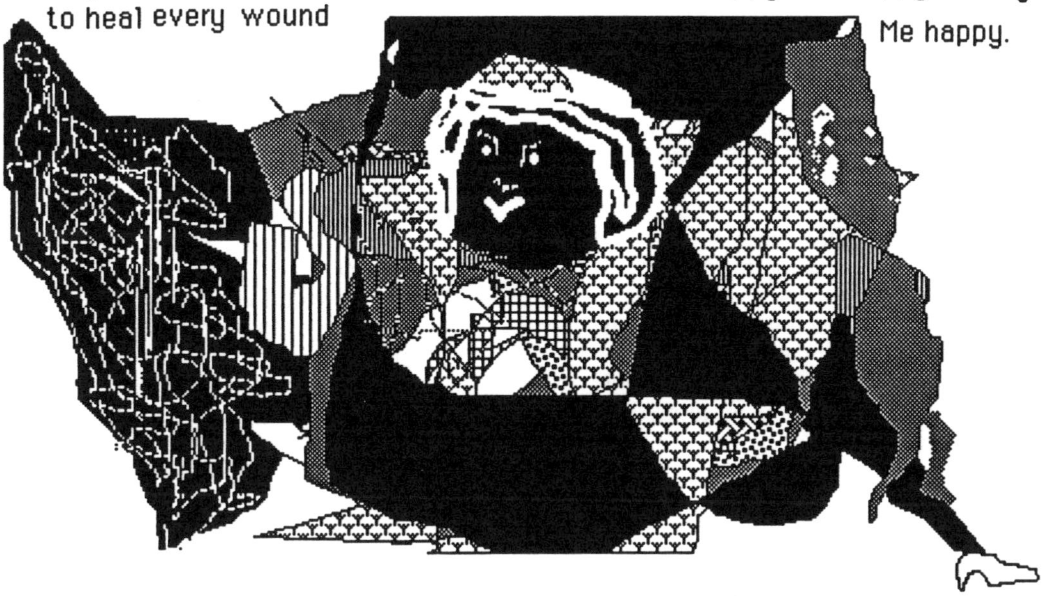

Words & Designs to Nudge a mind
6

HEART'S DESIGN

Life's Lesson #5 -
The Importance of Being Earnest

Watch the clock as it watches you.

Don't waste energy.

Plan all you want. God sends you a different itinerary in the morning.

Are you fluent in kindness? You will find others who speak the same language. at your doorstep.

Much that is called success
is a hurricane passing through.

In school they teach you the **5 senses**.
For that is all that they permit.
But in your heart **countless senses**
come to you, awesome, untutored, asking
you to play.

Many people boasting
a sense of humor have
betrayed their sense of decency.

Only in privacy does man
Suffer without smiling.

Flirt with words. What astonishing things
they say. Just now **they said**:
"Smell the **incense**
without becoming **incensed**.

"Let me **try**" - is ambitious.
" I'll **try** to" - is not.

"**SECRETS**" grow in shady spots.
Good ones should be nurtured
that way.
Bad ones brought to the light.

The best fortune arrives by
accident, on a Godly wind.

Review the dictionary.
How many words hold value for you?
Cross out the rest.

It takes a lifetimeto know what the blessings are.

Rewards too quickly received are soon forgotten or lead you astray.

Each moment of life is a gateway to destiny. Those examining the moment find a golden key.

All is illusion. Rewards are punishments. Punishments contain rewards. In either case if you know how to look at life neither one will lead you off your path.

Be wary of cliche speakers. They cover themselves with fuzzy thinking, offering danger to others as if they were sweets.

What are the great rewards of life?
In your answer notice they aren't manmade .
But forever changing and challengeing
simple and satisfying.
Subtly begun and modestly grown.

The flavors of life

Bitter, Sweet, Sour, Salty, Burnt.
Mix them, heat them, share them
and the recipe succeeds.

Talk to animals and find out
about yourself.
Look in their eyes and read what's there.

Language is composed to communicate.
Be a language.

If you want something bad enough
you will start the right action now.

Spare the child and spoil the rod.

Precise thought is patched together over time. Like the Abraham Lincoln antique ax where the handle had been replaced 5 times and the head 8 or 9. **Vintage Lincoln**.

It's alright

if you make a mistake
it's alright ...
maybe it's not a mistake but a new idea. -
Think about it.

LESSON #5 IMPORTANCE OF BEING EARNEST

You have only to recognize your innate power to create and attract treasures to receive them.

Every experience you encounter is a gift. The more valuable ones are called "bad luck".

Look at the little things that pop into your life -the key chains.You are the key that opens the doors.

Getting started is the hardest.
Staying there you gripe and groan.
But stick to it without glue,
And in time you'll come thru
And feel your work in a different tone.

The giving is the getting.
and vice versa.

God put his stately time pellets within you. these are activated by your passion and vision.. At the right moment it blooms in your bosom and another's. Your paths meet. Much in common ., communicating, giving, receiving, helping, joyful, coming from what you planted within, lo these many months or years. At the moment that you pray to God for the right way to be, the pellet pops into motion. Miracles begin.

Do not believe all the voices running through your head

Demand from them a shibboleth
confirming **LIFE** instead.
If they cannot do it , don't let them dwell within.
For they can prove that Heaven is Hell.
and Life is but a sin.
Bring out your good thoughts to pursue them
Till they leave the scene with dread.
Do not believe all the voices running through your head.

From nothing create something.
Be still when you can't do good.
Be joyful in your heart .
Don't gossip about the neighborhood.
Stay the course whether sick or lonely.
Don't believe bad words .
Invent good.actions independent of everyone else.
Have courage to climb the mountain in front of you.
Swim the river you must cross.
Be still in dangerous company.
Trust In God .
Let others prove themselves.
Good images make good days.

The more trials up the mountain, the more joy at the summit.

Your work will flourish

Your thoughts will nourish.
Just have courage
To stay the path.
Don't believe in words of fear.
See only that you stay sincere.
Do good works, be of good cheer.
Stay the path.
Wait with faith , Be ever kind.
Whatever good visions you feed to your mind
Wait for you around the bend.
Stay the Path.

BLESS THE BLESSINGS

Watch the blessings
Write them down
Many greet you this day.
Do not forget even one
For these forge the pearls of your smile.

THE ELEVENTH COMMANDMENT

Divide your day as God intended
Go to sleep when day has ended
Wake you up when sun is due
Work your work and have fun too.
Keep your faith, diminish fears
Life is seldom what it appears
Spread your love, wipe up anger
Keeps away undue danger
Blessed you will be, my friend
If you keep life a wholesome blend.
A simple smile, a glint of hope
Will always let you and others cope
On life's slippery slope.
If your day was spent worth while
You will fall asleep seeing God's smile.

Hang in. I'm coming.
Yeah.
Pleeez I beg you for God sake...
nooo heyyy.
!

OASIS FOUR: languages

it isn't the words
it's the music.
it isn't just you
and another person
connecting
It's the surprise of
gifting and gathering.

STRUCTURE

BUILD IT UP (breathe it in)

Tear it down!

BUILD ANOTHER (breathe it in)

Tear it up!

KEEP BUILDING
KEEP BREATHING

KEEP TEARING!!

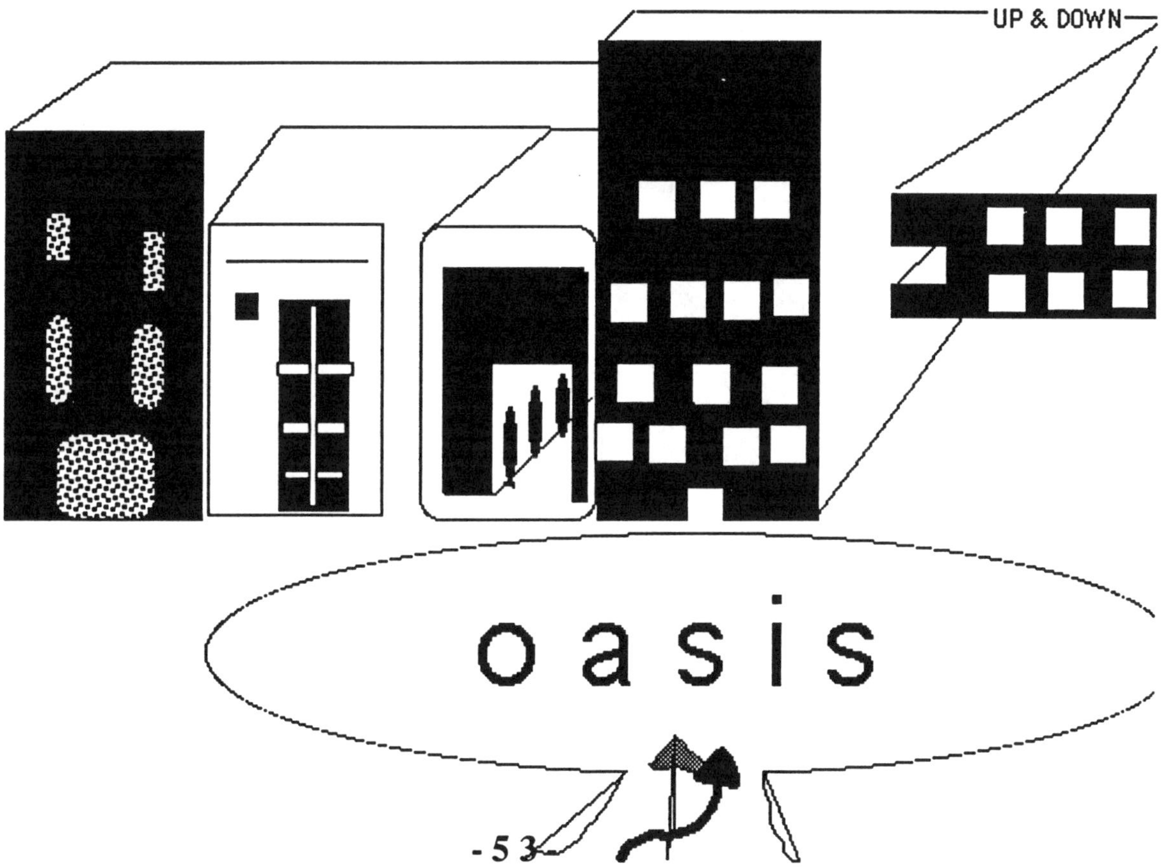

PORTUGUESE FORTUNES

SABES TU QUE...?

FORTUNAS QUE VOUS DEVRAIS CONNAITRE

1. Les mots sont toujours opportunistic.
   Les yeux, seul, disent la vérité.

2. L'homme change l'histoire s'accorder
   avec le publique.

3. Quoi que vous disiez, l'orielle
   l'entendre dire á sa façon.

4. Vous profitez de suivre votre
   instinct.

5. Guardez le troisième oeil ouvret
   quand on sommeile.

6. Beaucoup de jeux jouer,
   quelques uns gagneraient.

7. Les simples reactions déjouer
   l'avidité d'un autre.

8. Votre tête te blessé le cogniando
   contre le mur. Change la
   direction.

9. Suívez l'homme qui n'en veut rien.
   Il a tout

10. Fortune est un cheval féroce. Tiens vite
    pour le dompter.

11. La inquietude fait les bruits haut
    pendant que la réalité marcher
    en dedans sur la pointe des
    pieds.

Translation: Gérard Métayer

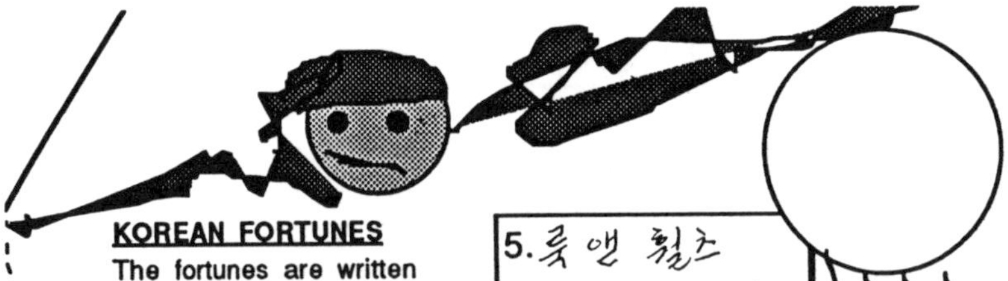

KOREAN FORTUNES

The fortunes are written in Korean phonetics. Ask a Korean to read the fortunes aloud to you. You will understand it instantly without translation.

1. 어브 올 더 메디신슨 러브 웍스 더 베스트

2. 투라이 투 화인드 더 뷰우티 인 이-취 펄슨. 잇 덴 이즈 유어즈

3. 비짓 네이추어. 쉬 윌 리스토어 유어 퍼훽트 밸런스

4. 어 굳 월드 앰브래이시스 텐 피플. 브링잉 그레이스 투 잇스 스피커.

5. 룩 앳 훨츠 드루어 텔레스콥 앤드 앳 버츄스 위드 어 마이크로스코프

6. 스테이 위드 그레이시어스 도우트 올 데이 앤드 유 윌 스테이 헬시.

7. 렛츠 노 디스트-랙숀. 킾 유 후럼 인너 사이렌스.

8. 어 카인드 월드 해즈 메디씨널 밸류 휘 잇츠 오너 앤드 리씨피앤트.

KOREAN FORTUNES 2

9. 어 후리 핫-트 캔 온리 러브.

10. 크리에이트 체인지스 인 유어 온 핫-츠 훠 어 베터 월-드.

11. 스터디 내추어 훠 디스 이즈 더 퍽추어 북 후럼 갇.

12. 미스테리 롸이시즈 휀 더 텅 라이스 스틸.

Korean Transliteration by Un Yong Yi

13. 프랜 어 해드 풋 인투 잇 스위트 앤드 애로-매릭 오일스.

14. 투 마치 인텔리젼스 캔 디스플레이스 더 하트

15. 완스 업온어타임 유 워본, 하우 훠처 냇츠 훠더 월드.

16 더 모어 유 컨화이드 인 내이추어 더 모어 쉬 컨화이즈 인 유.

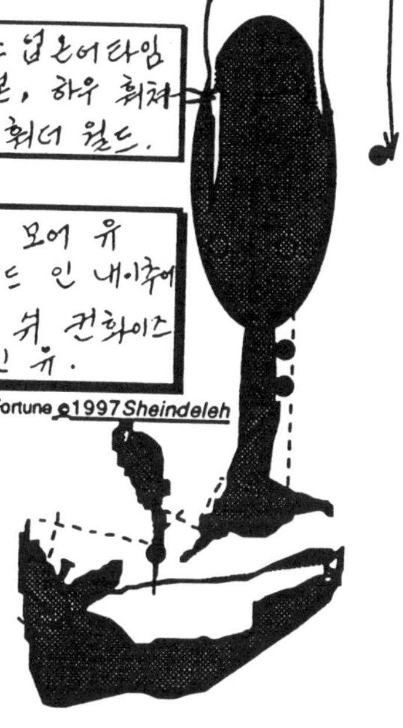

OBSchizzo FORTCHUNADOS (an invented language) * ©1997 Sheindeleh

FORCHUNADOS óBSCHíZZóS
To be read aloud away from the crowd.
To be understood without going to school.
To inspire and goad and tickle your fancy.
To make your head light and your breath full.

1. Ent dem clotheset shtandsa maiddel. Shtandest dere fun dem grave oop fon dem cradle. Viggle Viggle yu bist lüking endam shpigel. Crose duh door unddenyu vont C dot no mohr. Yuvish ent yugest it.

To speak Obschizzo like a native:

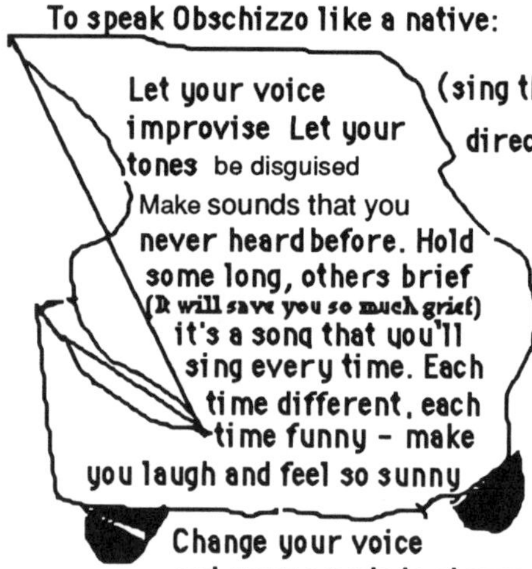

(sing these directions)

Change your voice and your words to change your world.

Timski poozl zundug,Mundug, Freetug
E pootz verts in dem bookses.
Mit mi E sez nodink. Unlee poozzl
E dawks to. Me no vait do pencil doon.
Me voyagia. Bye bye bebe.

Lishenski flenski cas ah yenski.
Braba babba skees ahaba.
Inta kinsta. Arsta kinsten.
Chande tzu? ... claacc... claacc.

Oskrusa vent
tzu shvern.
Der mestin in

lernen und
gesturest
Kin du unsta?

Parond enlox foodishan.

From a dream * Alternate languages presented themselves. I chose one and saw its bones glisten beige beneath gold. Whatever sound it was they or I made, produced twinkling eyes and nourishing laughter. No rules existed for we were free. Spoke without knowing. Heard without sound. The bubbling brook flows thru our hearts .. Join us and share your own language. **Sheindeleh**

Lolly tu vincheski.
Mnemoni .reski 'n
filgaroo fust danenos.
Spiritu craspeest
natuoda y prode.

Close micknice. fleech ich fiche.
Trent tvais
Senostra plais
Maa Maa , Paa paa. Cccook
coooccc Kooocc
C cuk-kahooo-ooo-wwww-wah.

Get out of your shell.
Learn obschizzo.
Use your God given voices to read sing circuitously and listen to the many voices you are capable of

Use the white space to add your own Obschizzo Forchunados.

Scuzi fluzi
stuggi minnuzi
braaavasteh
laaaranda aaaah

Mini moni mani
midina fila fanni
drat tum pan
faa raa raa raa ra.

'allo 'allo 'allo
Bnist tomki
Bnist lusk
Bnist fro'
Blist y Bro'

Skata jej
Skata mej
Skata hemnes
Pi Pa Po.

Ich res waski
Tus embent
Vis albraski
Kum sa mer.

Haaaaaaaaaaaa hoooooooooo hiiiiiiiiiiiiiiiiii
heyyyyyyyyyyy huuuuuuuu haay heee haaaa
shaaaaaaaaaah shuh

LSN TO ME I GOT SUM DING TO TLYU HOKAY?

Regino Laspi crapask den filso..

Mrando
Flando
Poosh
Dein
Grando.

Ven tings free den tings Ah crezy. Payoop dis is gootfah mi entfah yu- meks pippl luf iitch uder in ah gutn veh. Nut too mooch to mek vun hepP.Greety pple kill gulden guse. Simple simbl sempre sane. Fine your muse y B hopP.

Yesterd
ay vlant
Today
vlint.
Tomorro
vlock.
Why not
pursue?

Collaborative Fill in song:
Plazee plez ____
Mahmee fr____
Du showst ___
_____ kim poh
S_____boy_____
Koo _____ ____
______ ____ tu
Feen ______
Cha zhaaa____
Ah ha ha ha ha
(2X) ______ ___
____
____

Your friskt menash
popped. Ant mine
la di dah stopped. klip
dein chin prop up.

La shaz farr distinza.finza minza
Velsta mura.pura cura
Bunestra creesta.meesta. reesta
Imgrocka flaaa.
aha aha ha ha ha.
Haaaaaaaaa. Haaaaa. Haaaa.

ARABIC FORTUNES

These fortunes are written phonetically in Arabic
Find a person who can read Arabic. What you hear will be English.

فور أيفري أوك ورد سكسس ذير آر ١٠٠٠ أنور دونز

أف يو كانت كيب يور برامسس ما كيب ذم تو يورسلف.

سايلنس أز ذا هوم أوف ميركلز

ايز سو تتشنك فور كولد بيكم هارد.

أيتشي مان ازهز اون كراجس.

برتند ويل أنيف أند ذا تروث ويل أدابت تو أت.

Translation into Arabic: Mohamad

Y IDDISH Fortunes ©1988 SHEINDELEH

(Zie Du Nisht Fahrzorgt, Ahs Mit Yiddish Mehn Kehn Maken Als Frailach)

1. Di zorgen du host ist fun nechtig.
   Heint dem zin machst varm.
2. Yeden tracht macht ah molecule.
3. Ah kleinem vort ken maken dem leben shlect ober gidt.
4. Ahs du vilst epis krigen
   mos du batzoln mit ah tracht.
5. Ahs gelt gefelt, mos men tzien mit dem hartz.
6. Koif nit verten vos makt du mishugeh.
7. Min koift, min loift un lost gefalen a friendt.
8. Dein verten vet tzurick kumen en dein kiseneh.
9. Ah laiben maint tzu gaiben.
10. Du host alles en dein kop tzu maken ah gut yor.
11. Gibt tzu allemen tzu redn mit dem hartz.
12. Ahs menchen zein shlect tzu dir, du zie gidt, un dos vet aribergain.
13. Ahs du vilst vos du vilst, vest du krigen.
14. Di zin vet kumen, di fligel vet zingen far dir.
15. Far dir, epis gidt vet zingen heint.
16. If only our hearts translated into others, love would be easy.
17. Fun yeden mench loift ah yingeleh.
18. Zog nidt vos du zaist. Zog vos is gidt.
19. Nemt arop dem oigen fun anderen menchen. Du host altz.
20. Dem vos vaist gornisht, lozst verten rinen fun dem mohl.
21. Redt nit vile du est ahs dem verten vel essen dir.

Unas fortunas Espanol ©1997 Sheindeleh

Él quien sabe todo,
Aprende nada más.

Camina con el viento.
Te secas tus lagrimas

Habla en silencio una hora al dia
para méjor salud.

Las relaçiones: 50-50 es haburido.
Mejor: 150-158.
La mas mejor: "Quien cuenta?"

Acuesta en la cama. Un problema
en tue mente, se te caera mientras
tu duerme.

Translated by : Juan Manuel Baéz

Tu eres más fortunado que 18%.
de la populaçion No me cree?
Ver los necrológicos de ayer.

La alegria se te puede correr.
Si te estas quieto, te alcansara.

Más afortunado que siendo rico?
Teniento riquisa.

Por bajo de cada recompensa
que se seduce está atado un castigo
secreto. La una está la otra.

Escucha la musica.
Podemos llorer en qualquiere
tiempo.

Invierno-Frio: Demasiada   personas
no estan usando una sonriza de verano.

Scratch a certainty and you will find doubt. keep digging at the doubt and you will find certainty. There you go what you suspected all along:::doubts lead to

OASIS 5

PARADOX

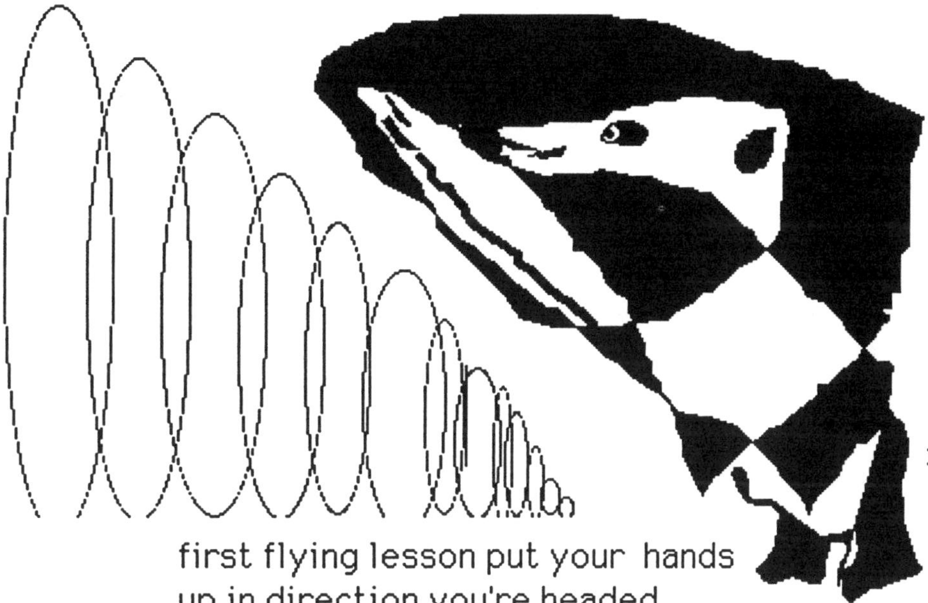

CERTAINTY

and

that leads to doubts.

LIFE is PARADOX.

first flying lesson put your hands up in direction you're headed.

knowledge vs.innocence

innocent knowledge

PARADOX ○ ○ ○ PARADOX

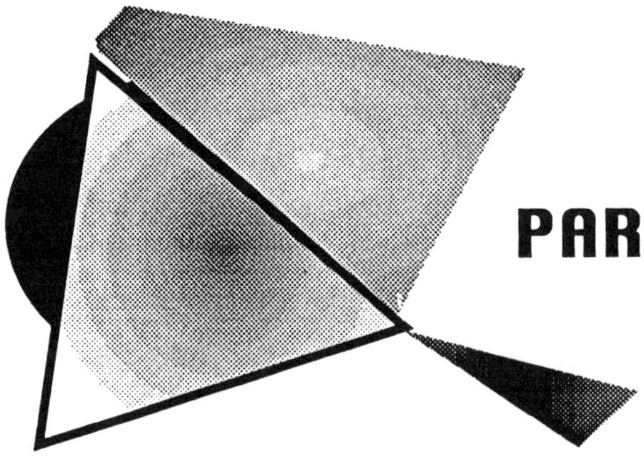

PARADOX 1

What is IT that has no shadow yet leaves one.
Has no substance - and fills the air.
Has little duration, but endures a lifetime.
IT is without physicality. Yet the majority hold onto IT.
Kings and paupers access IT in huge amounts without cost.
People sacrifice a generous portion of IT to friends and strangers.
When they receive IT in return, they discard IT .
IT is used as protection, worn with grace or wantoness
Small applications of IT miraculously heal, while too large a dose destroys.
Some make use of IT properties to become a leader.
Others completely oblivious to IT's powers become toolbearers.
No matter where used, IT leaves after effects.
Once we touch IT, IT becomes our inheritance

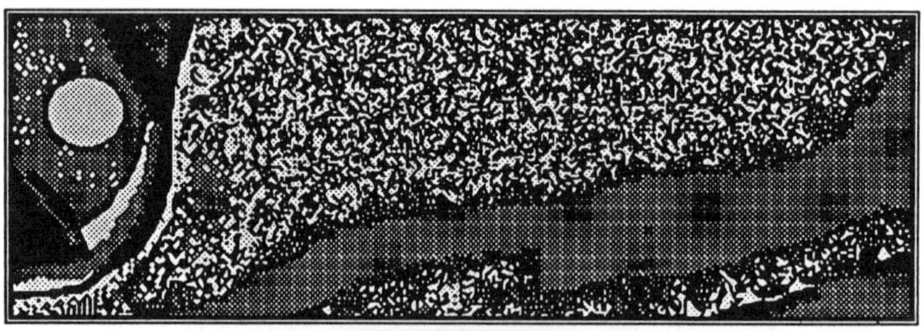

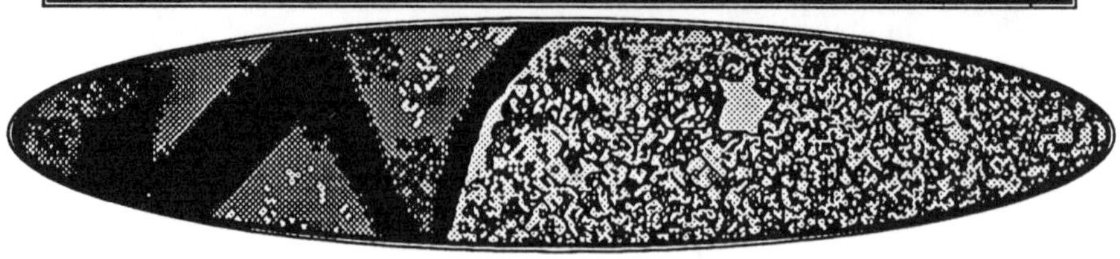

Feel its power. Do you know what IT is? Turn to page 66 to solve the puzzle.

PARADOX 2

What is the place?
Somewhere all seek yet seeing it, run from.

Flexible parameters can stand on any hill or valley.
Withstand natural disasters

It's immensity can be folded down to the invisible.

It is sacred to the mind and profane in action.

A glimpse heals, a judgement befouls.

Getting there requires no money. Remaining one begets a fortune.

Camouflaged by light. It is dazzling in the night.

The form changes - the inhabitants weep
With joy or wistfulness

Search but you will not find it. Look away, it reveals itself.

Do you know what this place is? The truth of the solution lies on page 67.

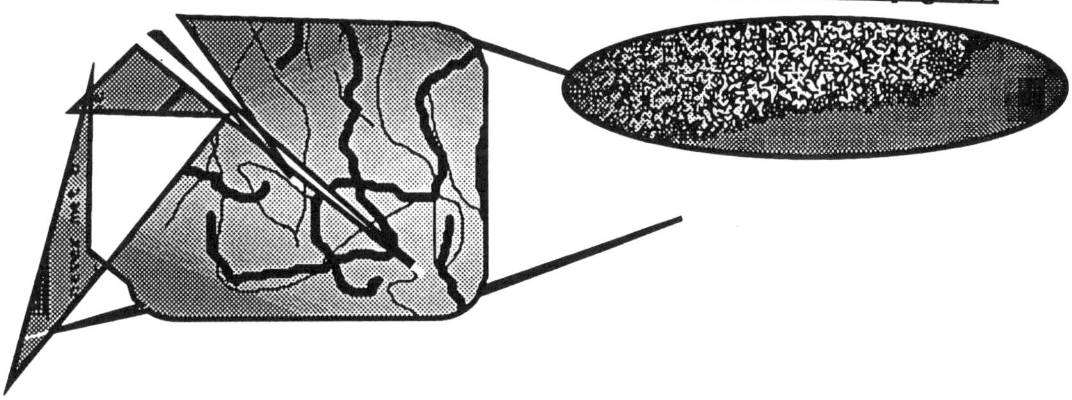

SOLUTION TO THE PARADOX

Figure out the clues. Circle or color the letters.
Unscramble the remaining letters to find the mysterious "IT".

1.Love is ----- you find it.
2.---- is what you make it.
3.-- as I say not as I --.
4.A stitch in ---- saves nine.

H	O	T	E	L	E
O	D	O	R	D	R
M	E	H	I	T	E
E	F	I	W	D	W

SOLUTION: "IT" is ____ ____

Solution

I

SOLUTION TO THE PARADOX II

Figure out the clues. Circle or color the letters. Unscramble the remaining letters to find the mysterious 'PLACE"

1. KEEP YOUR DESK IN GOOD ----- AND YOUR WORK IMPROVES.
2. GET OUT TODAY AND ENJOY THE SUN. ALL ---- AND NO ----MAKES JOHNNY A DULL BOY. 3. HANG IN THERE. ---- IS ON THE WAY.
4. SOMEONE YOU --- A LONG TIME AGO COMES BACK INTO YOUR LIFE.

H	L	A	P	L	W
O	O	T	R	K	E
M	R	O	L	D	R
E	E	P	V	Y	E

SOLUTION: "IT' is ________

II

Paradox 3

SECRETS

If you hold a secret too long everyone knows it.

Secrets change hands and once they do a new secret is born.

Some secrets are sweet when blended with caffeine.

Everyone who has a **Secret**

has a secret agenda.

If you do not tell people your secrets, they will make them up for you.

If your secrets are not exciting enough

they will embellish them without charge.

You torture yourself by asking someone to keep a secret for you. Far better to say " Tell all your friends if you think it might make you more popular." For that is surely what will happen. Even better, go buy yourself a microphone & broadcast it. Nobody will pay attention

or remember it.

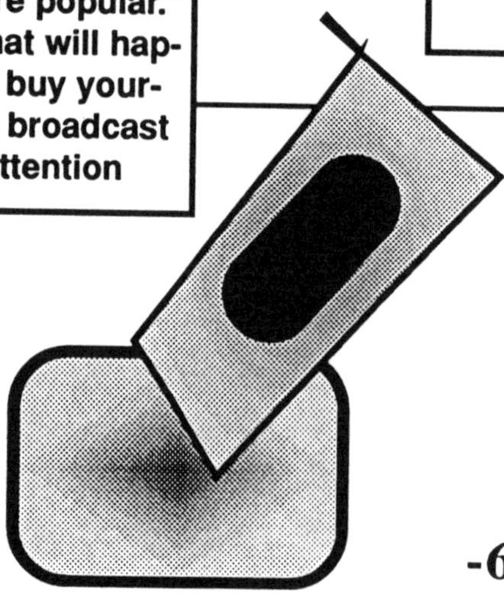

WHAT IS THIS THING CALLED?

PARADOX 4

A VALUABLE COMMODITY

You can't get it until you give it.
You can't give it until you have it.
You can't have it until you find it.
You can't find it until you're quiet.
You can't be quiet until you're alone

You won't be alone until you accept loneliness.
When you accept loneliness you will be alone
And then you will be quiet.

When you are quiet
You will find it.
when you find it you will have it.
When you have it you will give it.
When you give it you will get it.

When you get it, you will share it.
when you share it you will get more of it.
When you get more of it
you will be still more quiet.

When you are still more quiet you will
get it give it and understand it
in a profound way.

Solution is on page 70

P A R A D O X

To the quiet observer all life is a paradox or conundrum.
The words that should elucidate are sheaved in deception.
The gut feeling, wordlessly prods us with its truth.

Paradox　　Solution 4

Color or circle the letters of the clues. unscramble the remaining letters to solve the Paradox

M	U	S	T	D
O	T	A	K	P
R	A	V	E	L
E	H	E	R	L

SOLUTION: "IT" is ▢▢▢▢ ▢▢▢▢

CLUES

1. ATLAS is famous for its variety of - - - - with much information for travelers.

2. Some people are shy and don't like to - - - - much.

3. A sheep dog is used to round up the - - - - and keep them from wandering off.

OASIS SIX: Interactive fortunes (incluudes 16,000,000 Customized Fortunes)

Collaborate with these
And your mind will ease

Your question will be answered
Your heart & mind will understand.

Gotta get pair of jockeys
Wait for me.
Hang in. I'm coming.
Yeah.
Pleeez I beg you for God sake...
nooo heyyy.

BLIND-SIGHT[M] ©1997 Sheindeleh

It is possible for you to match 4800 custom fortunes with your question. Ask a personal or philosophical question. Do not ask a YES or NO question. Choose one of the printed phrases randomly. You may do this by saying a number first, then locating the phrase or by putting your finger directly on a phrase. Have a blind friend who can read braille do the same using the braille pages in the center of the book. The two phrases thus chosen create a custom fortune.

THERE ARE 40 BRAILLE PHRASES AND 40 PRINTED PHRASES.

Your fortune will be one of a possible 1600 separate fortunes. This amount can be increased by adding a third phrase from either list, and increased more by adding a fourth phrase. And the more ways you can interweave the phrases or partial phrases the larger the total will be. It's more fun and there are more dynamics working from both lists with a braille partner. However if a partner is currently unavailable use your own list to choose two printed sayings to get your custom fortune(s). Bonne chance! *Sheindeleh*

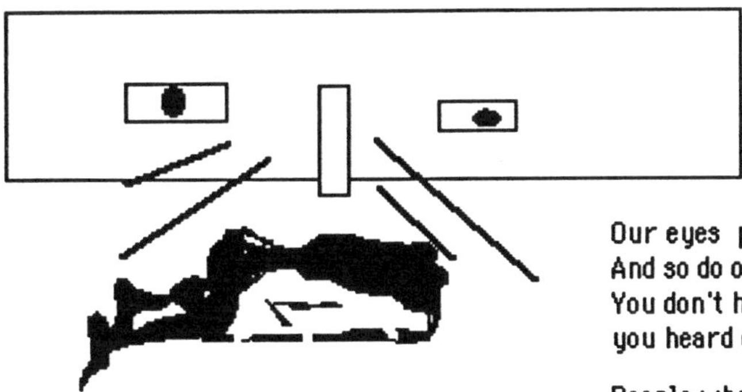

Our eyes play tricks on us
And so do our lies
You don't hear what you think
you heard or see what you say you saw.

People who fight about this are
wasting their energy.

It isn't against the law (yet)
to pretend you heard something
else or saw something
exquisite.

For it is the law of some universes
that what you say, is a tool
for happiness or sadness,
↖ (your choice). ↗

Obey the law.

BLIND-SIGHT M ©1997 Sheindeleh

1. Upon awakening
2. A new lifestyle
3. Events softly unfold.
4. Answer arrives soon.
5. Strange gifts.
6. Tranquil solution.
7. Stoke the furnace.
8. special friends
9. Learn something new.
10. A correct hunch
11. with action
12. with faith
13. many clues.
14. the time is right.
15. at the right time.
16. Stay alert.
17 Meticulous planning
18. What you want.
19. Simplify
20. Early start helps.

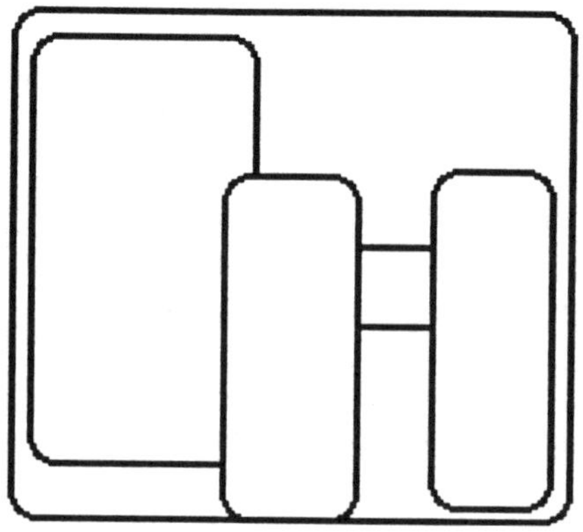

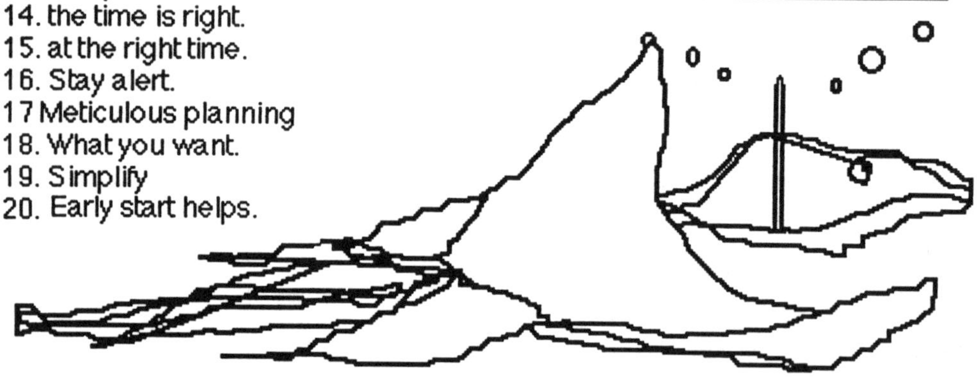

If you're programmed you know the name of everything. Break through programming and you will not know it. Silence has as many variations as music. When you make silence you are a silencesician.

Once you practice and know your craft you may play with the greatest musicians to elicit the profoundest emotions.

BLIND SIGHT (21-40)

21. Fragile thoughts
22. immediate rewards.
23. Something's necessary.
24. All avenues
25. Wait until dark
26. Symbols open enigmas
27. Through every impulse
28. Present situation improves.
29. Deja Vu or something new.
30. response is wonderful.
31. consequences.
32. Another way works.
33. Foolishness can be avoided.
34. Face yourself.
35. Make position clear.
36. Chit Chat is uplifting.
37. Physically.
38. before you speak.
39. Feet on the ground.
40. Stay in the middle.

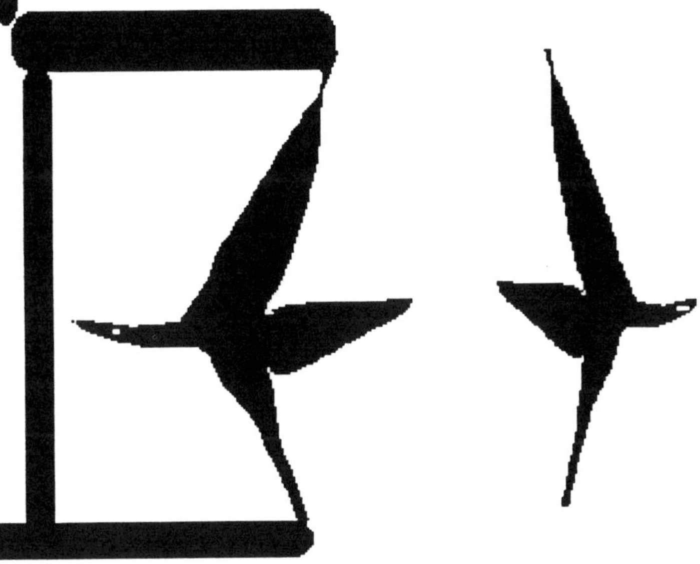

The world isn't what you think. Think
You're never stuck in one place. Placebo.
Lights have switches. Switch.
Laughing sucks up the hairballs. Have a ball.
You're allowed to laugh at nothing at all. All.

Where'd everyone go?

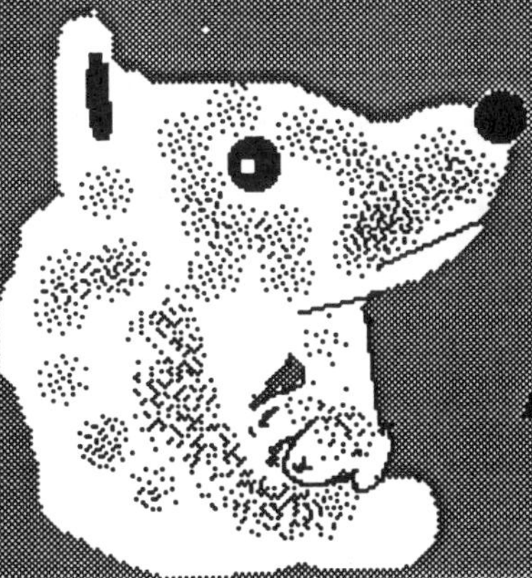

ACRONYMS

COUNTLESS

FORTUNES

Bring out answers **E**asily let letters **A**ttract the answers which **R**eside in the spirit resisting logic.

Barriers crumble Enigmas fall Altercations bend Resistance stops

All letters
Create mood, motive, and action.
Requests for answers
Open your mind
Nudge you into a broader outlook
Your focusing on acronyms
Manipulates millions of concepts
Sensing the real, the magic, and
the roads leading to each.

ACRONYMS

Follow a line or pop around and pick 3.
? = your choice.

ASK A QUESTION (open ended) or **ASK FOR A MESSAGE**
Choose 3 letters. These letters will fit your request
See what words you get from them. Play with your choice.

TRADE THE WORDS until they make you laugh or gasp with recognition.

COUNTLESS FORTUNES

the MENTOR YES NO MAYBE

Ask a YES or NO question. Point to a number on this page.
Locate the number on pages 2 - 5 for your answer.

94	40	54	23	59	4	73	37	19	20
17	65	22	58	61	53	84	14	9	83
85	3	29	95	72	69	46	18	60	27
16	45	91	7	62	6	33	30	92	13
35	82	74	2	28	100	87	25	98	80
99	15	64	89	31	21	70	26	12	5
11	71	1	32	34	56	48	36	86	77
8	52	43	93	24	47	41	57	88	49
66	78	38	51	76	44	50	10	96	75
39	81	54	90	67	68	42	63	97	79

If you land here, you get the bonus number

Bonus number.........> 101

This randomness of choice leads to surprises. It triggers new ways to look at your questions. If you act upon any answer which impresses you, this helps in bringing the fortune to fruition. Look back in a couple of weeks and check out available results. This is a method of strongly associating your thoughts to a seemingly random yet synchronious world. Sheindeleh
10/14/97

1. Now is the time to try men's souls with honesty, energy, commitment. YES.
2. There's strength in numbers.
   Don't go against popular opinion. MAYBE.
3. If you have tested the waters proceed. YES.
4. A little risk is fine but don't be fool hardy. MAYBE
5. Appearances are deceiving. You will do just fine. YES.
6. Make up your mind to focus on one major part of question and proceed. YES.
7. He who hesitates is boss. NO for now.
8. There's a place for you and your wishes. It is a unique situation. YES.
9. Look before you lead with your chin.
   Proceed with caution. MAYBE.
10. Spend a day meditating.
    The answer will pop out at you. MAYBE.
11. They often "kill the messenger".
    Find other supports first. NO.
12. A bit of role playing with mental mentors will assure you. YES
13. Become thorougly grounded before making attempt.
    Wait if not sure. MAYBE.
14. Break the boundaries of previous attempts.
    Be daring. YES.
15. Your ego has you off-center. Attend to this first.
    For now the answer is NO.
16. Stop playing games.
    Is this question necessary? MAYBE.
17. This situation could be huge success.
    Keep it close to chest. YES.
18. Only your gut feeling counts.
    Don't be too anxious. MAYBE
19. Find an action that connects you to honest people. YES.
20. Each question is its own answer.
    What answer are you asking? MAYBE.
21. The genre is predicated from each seed .
    Look back at the seed. Keep nurturing. YES.
22. Further aggressive efforts takes you in an unrewarding direction. Stop now. NO.

23. Proceed calmly and joyfully.
It goes well. YES.
24. Permit yourself to smile and exhale.
Continue in direction you've been going. YES.
25. It's your faith that makes the plan feasible.
Continue at your leisure. YES.
26. Many experiences led you here. You're at the crossroads.
If there is no lingering doubt, the answer is YES.
Otherwise review question at another time.
27. Resistance to your plans was in the past.
If you're ready, continue in gradual manner. YES.
28. Something at this time is working against this. Wait. NO.
29. Find someone as a sounding board for these thoughts and plans. MAYBE.
30. The heights can be dizzying and cold. Prepare yourself mentally and spiritually first. MAYBE
31. Get your materials in order. Visualize proceedures and possibilities. If this is confirmed in your mind, proceed. YES.
32. Nothing comes from haste but waste. A few days to review and improve puts you in a better position. NO for now.
33. All roads lead you up. YES.
34. More than you realize, there are mentors to your needs.YES.
35. Point for point investigate where this leads.
You have to change something. MAYBE
36. Forward, March and get your rewards. YES.
37. Why so sudden? Is it just boredom escaping ennui? NO.
38. Persistence pays off. YES.
39. It's a question of timing. Keep navigating. MAYBE.
40. Reality sets in soon. And you flow with it. YES.
41. Day by day it comes closer to culmination.
Your attitude is correct. YES.
42. Why not? Only you can say. MAYBE.
43. There's a better way. Brainstorm.
Make an Einstein thought experiment. NO.
44. Sanity reigns. Take proper steps to reach a solution. NO.
45. Help reaches you in two days to make this more solid. NO.
46. Entrance or Exit? How good does it feel in your gut.
This is your call. MAYBE.
47. It's great. Jump in. YES.

48. No blame. No shame. Try again. NO.
49. Destiny is on a parallel with your efforts. YES.
50. Escalate your communication with outside forces. YES.
51. Let serendipity take it from here. YES.
52. Earthbound you can't do it.
Let your plans include fantasy. MAYBE.
53. Happiness is natural when you're on track.
Are you on track? MAYBE.
54. Favors must be reciprocated. MAYBE.
55. Remember your friends. Roll with the punches. NO.
56. Yesterday and today give tomorrow's actions. MAYBE.
57. Widen your point of view. NO.
58. One answer to everything you ask. YES.
59. Garner the energy. Proceed without procrastinating. YES.
60. Upside down answers are frustrating your completion.
Straighten them out. NO.
61. You need insights to see the road ahead. Get them and go. NO.
62. Opposites must be utilized. It will boggle the mind. NO.
63. Hints of the unseen are needed to proceed.
Allow them to come at their will to you. MAYBE.
64. Evolution will provide revolution you require. NO.
65. Answers are coming. Sleep on it.
Tomorrow you act on it.YES.
66. Laughter releases tension. This is key to the question. MAYBE.
67. Patience. Patience. Patience. NO.
68. Options are available.
They are all aides in your endeavor. YES.
69. Promise yourself the next step and do it. YES.
70. Vacillation. There's a tiny fly in the ointment.
Seek it out. Get rid of it. NO.
71. Yes! Unequivocally and absolutely. Yes!. YES.
72. Easy going. Piece of cake. Your call. YES.
73. Applause for your highest efforts. YES.
74. Leave go of useless mind chatter and worry.
Then reconsider options. NO.
75. Long awaited results come easily and quickly. YES.
76. Imagination helps this to succeed. YES.
77. Nice situation emerging. Congratulations. YES.
78. Place to go now is out. Rest the thinking faculties.YES.

79. Escalate daily decisions. But hold off on this one. MAYBE.
80. Rusty keys don't open doors. Find a good locksmith. NO.
81. Shape your world with your vision. YES.
82. Only one more step to make it. NO for now.
83. Next time work without fears. NO.
84. Face new issues. New factors have crept in. MAYBE.
85. High ideals could work for your agenda. MAYBE.
86. Easy does it. Time to de-escalate. Come in for landing. YES.
87. Respect all the forces.
Re-examine what you're doing. MAYBE.
88. Each nail makes your position more secure.
Drive a few more home. NO.
89. Opposites attract.
Look in unlikely corners for allies. YES.
90. Kiss it off. Make a detour. NO.
91. Some like it hot. Some like it cold. Investigate. NO.
92. Every day has added fuel to this fire.
It's ready for the pot. YES.
93. Singular events have positioned you to proceed. YES.
94. A hundred different ways to go but only three hold promise. Try them.YES.
95. Life hands you conundrums which you must make sense of. If you like these riddles you'll solve the present one easily. YES.
96. Raise your expectations, lower your temperature.
You have the answer. YES.
97. An unlikely force pulls you into the correct path.
Keep going. YES.
98. Keep your eye on the ball.
Run the bases. You make a home run. YES.
99. Sloppy thinking. Focus more - make corrections. Until then NO.
100. There's an art to successfully climbing Mt. Sisyphus. Most importantly, avoid the rock's entering or landing upon your brain. Change lanes to get to new range. When you reach the top enjoy a brief respite before returning to ground level where a new and nobler rock waits for you. **YES.**
101. With all your heart set out to accomplish this.
YESYESYESYESYESYESYESYES No maybe's about it

To find their fortune
Where'd everyone go?

16,000,000 CUSTOMIZED FORTUNES

FOR YOUR DINING PLEASURE

210 phrases on each tray for mixing, matching and contemplating.

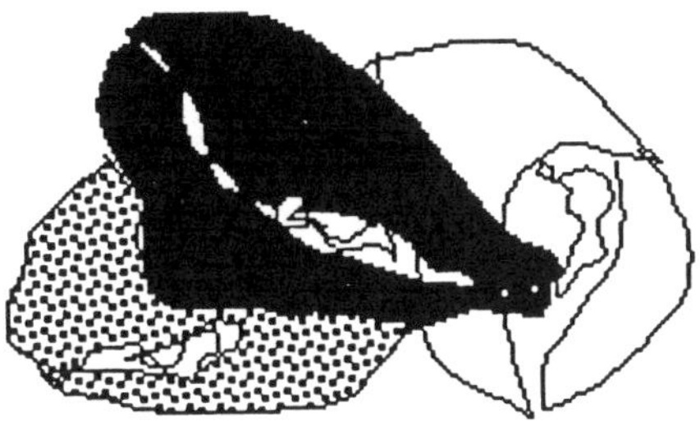

One can be quite filling OR
You can chew on as many
as you want. Your heart will
never go hungry.

CUSTOMIZED FORTUNES
created and written by
Sheindeleh

16,000,000 CUSTOMIZED FORTUNES SM © 1997 Sheindeleh

CUSTOMIZED FORTUNESSM may seem amazing but we do it all the time in ordinary thinking, changing our thoughts with different combinations of words. When we get bogged down with problems we have only one way to look at the world. We cannot see a way out. **CUSTOMIZED FORTUNES**SM clears the path to unclog the area where we feel stuck offering a wide vista for solutions and confirms the places where we have made progress.

Ask a question or mention a topic you are concerned with: personal, world or philosophical. Mentally, choose **3** numbers from 1 to **210**, one for each column. Then read your **Customized Fortunes**SM.

1. Today's problem	1. leads to joy	1. when you smile at another.
2. Notice the change	2. All will turn out well	2. outside and in.
3. You need only	3. stay placid	3. You meet a good person.
4. Will power	4. valuable info. flows	4. for true love.
5. Serendipity	5. intuitively	5. catch the wave
6. Freedom calls	6. fulfill a grand idea	6. nourishing day
7. Keep going	7. Be who you are	7. charge up
8. Tomorrow	8. speak up	8. play fully
9. Your wishes	9. reveal who you are	9. Open the door.
10. Keep your promises	10. Point to treasures	10. in every situation.
11. You're destined to	11. leave others enriched	11. Transformation
12. Stay centered	12. reach a higher level	12. receive wisdom
13. Trust yourself	13. A rare opportunity	13. Miracles happen
14. Mentors	14. lots of choices	14. stirs your soul
15. Learn from mistakes	15. Blessings multiply	15. in a new arena.
16. Straight answers	16. hasten process	16. so be it.
17. Create atmosphere	17. returns to you.	17. A good laugh.
18. Dear friend	18. It shows up	18. and you're home free
19. Coincidence	19. reaps rewards	19. beyond what you imagine
20. Life's call	20. Your heart sings.	20. Your body vibrates.

CUSTOMIZED FORTUNES

#21-47

21. Conscience favors
22. Major mix up
23. recent events whisper
24. A small clue
25. Prepare to fly
26. likelihood of
27. grand plans
28. Get into gear
29. Reduce fears
30. Travel soon
31. Fragrant moment
32. Shine on.
33. Don't stop
34. Search mind
35. Pay closer attention
36. Exchange courtesy
37. Life flows
38. Believe it's so
39. Never doubt
40. Moving on
41. pretty up
42. combination thinking
43. Prayer works
44. Suddenly it occurs
45. Good thoughts
46. Gently pull out.
47. around the bend

21. tough answers
22. several ways
23. what a day
24. nail it down
25. reduced friction
26. brave success
27. faith must be held
28. signals
29. to harmonize
30. scatter waves
31. free up space
32. standing ovation
33. rescuing thoughts
34. perpetual motion
35. inner voices
36. charged thoughts
37. unexpected change
38. beautiful reward
39. the shining stars
40. personal triumphs
41. keep your cool
42. learn lesson
43. surprise yourself
44. superb event
45. finished product
46. reality check.
47. single answer

21. to simple questions.
22. stranger comes to the rescue
23. state of ecstasy.
24. hidden knowledge.
25. the right time to begin.
26. It's in your hands.
27. in 24 hours.
28. for a new journey.
29. with much relief.
30. bring a dream to reality.
31. in all aspects.
32. make it worthwhile.
33. friends will come.
34. major break through.
35. hunches pay off.
36. produces affinity.
37. continuing growth.
38. resembles last success.
39. flat out happiness.
40. "At last I'm free"
41. It gets better.
42. Gets you a million on the way up.
43. come to terms with situation.
44. comes to fruition.
45. check it out.
46. are you ready?
47. the first time.

Customized Fortunes

48 -73

48. Dream on
49. Be aware
50. Get a rain check
51. More benefits
52. Listen more
53. Stick around
54. Open heart
55. Raise funds
56. Great news
57. A big secret
58. This occurs
59. It's all good
60. New friend
61. Quite simply
62. Spend more time
63. Place your faith
64. Enough thinking
65. A certainty
66. A presentation
67. Resources
68. Stand by
69. Ignore negatives
70. Count on this
71. A frequent habit
72. All depends on you
73. There's more to it

48. time to go
49. saying truths
50. during the week
51. tap into common sense
52. to have dialogue
53. ask for what you need
54. gather together
55. prophetic joke
56. the next time
57. research helps
58. give it time
59. the answer lies deep within you.
60. Slow simmering
61. save energy
62. see more people
63. respect situation
64. with more spontaneity
65. more acceptance
66. You deserve more
67. make it happen
68. you'll know what to do.
69. for now
70. face facts
71. examine details.
72. Active imagination
73. if you wish

48. you'll find what you need.
49. life gets better then good.
50 chance event favors you.
51. keep secrets.
52. new information.
53. accent on goal.
54. enjoy the camaraderie.
55. keep the faith. It comes.
56. decisions are easier.
57. good results.
58. stop for now.
59. for the hundredth time.
60. for what you need.
61. let it out.
62. raise more questions.
63. with a bold reply.
64. enormous response.
65. act accordingly.
66. and you will get justice.
67. and you grow.
68. it's got to happen.
69. you meet amazing mentors.
70. fallacies disappear.
71. get rid of unnecessary minutiae.
72. it helps present situation.
73. make your choices.

Customized Fortunes #74-99

74. Dress up	74. put talent to work	74. watch **public reactions.**
75. judge not	75. cheer up	75. **full steam ahead.**
76. It gets better.	76. you will succeed	76. feel **wonderful.**
77. It's a snap.	77. loving environment	77. open door to good life.
78. joy comes.	78. what you worked for	78. is here to stay.
79. Drudgery ends.	79. if you've done the job	79. the rewards flow in.
80. play with work	80. keep smiling	80. gain happiness.
81 be aware	81. be patient	81. master creation.
82. there's time	82. Find the avenue	82. n a **humble way.**
83. take this chance	83. write a letter.	83. watch results.
84. your wishes	84 insert reality	84. everyone smiles.
85. when perplexed	85. when perplexed	85. resolution comes.
86. review events	86. blame no one	86. continue optimism.
87. final chance	87. stop games	87. honesty the answer.
88. song's message	88. reserve power there	88. by next Tuesday.
89. good quality	89. Proof comes	89. respect thy neighbor.
90. confusion teaches (& message 216)	90. fulfill obligations (& message 216)	90. find solutions. (& message 216)
91. Exceptional thoughts	91. restore order	91. with correct actions.
92. take the time	92. sample each idea	92. forget barriers.
93. whatever it takes (& message 210)	93. see it through (& message 210)	93. cast away doubts. (& message 210)
94. all you need do	94. lighten point of view	94. surprises (any bonus message)
95. sweet results	95. satisfaction guaranteed	95. persist in search.
96. every day	96. fake it, shake it, make it	96. reveal a reality.
97. don't panic	97. roll with punches	97. benefits accrue.
98. memory helps	98. new friends	98. rich laughter.
99. good rule	99. Love thyself diligently	99. in small & big ways.

Customized Fortunes

#100-126

100. Price is high
101. Learn how
102. Get out now
103. Put it away
104. set time lines
105. You'll know
106. Respect yourself
107. Potent tools
108. For God's sake
109. Be renewed
110. Wind up affairs
111. Subtle powers
112. Accustom yourself
113. No matter the circumstances
114. needed changes come.
115. Simple message
116. Lose some of your ego.
117. It will be wonderful
118. Three more days
119. stay firm
120. Don't lose temper
121. Resist quitting
122. Put down the script
123. Time exists for you
124. Pick your moment.
125. Traveling
126. Trust yourself

100. Everything is possible
101. you have opportunity
102. stop where you are
103. look up
104. create the vision
105. the answer
106. Pay attention
107. see what you're doing
108. enough already
109. stand up now
110. Fade out.
111. hinge on credibility
112. without hesitation
113. You and God
114. you - will - survive
115. take a new view
116. find the time.
117. to come into wealth
118. a beautiful experience
119. let the past go by.
120. use your humor
121. Hang-ups change.
122. Let the writing unfold
123. Two lovely experiences
124. Pick your action
125. See the nature of it.
126. See reality.

100. Attitude is leverage.
101. Anything goes.
102. resist absorption
103. let nothing stop you
104. do the next thing
105. right away
106. situation irons out
107. solution to problem
108. Feed yourself.
109. create movement
110. get into next scene.
111. be a leader
112. go with gut feelings.
113. will straighten it out.
114. God stays with you.
115. you have the key.
116. increases energy
117 without struggling.
118. The adventure begins
119. acknowledge the moment.
120. everyone benefits.
121. make sunbeams.
122. It touches the heart.
123. Express your heart
124. See it happen
125. Perhaps a victory.
126. Truth shines.

Customized Fortunes

#127-153

127. A hundred ways	127. without thought	127. the solution comes.
128. Your visions	128. supersede your fears	128. it exists now.
129. Things are things.	129 A heart has wings.	129. see what that brings.
130. Sometimes	130. don't struggle	130. have a cup of tea - talk to the muses.
131. Walk outside	131. with your heart still	131. someone talks to you.
132. Ignore bad words	132. see what God has wrought.	132. put your words to song.
133. Envision the good.	133. Chemical reaction.	133. you become a different person.
134. If you take time	134. Make a deep dream	134. you will know where to put your next step.
135. It's your journey	135. Pay the price.	135. your destiny is clear.
136. Any day is worthwhile	136. little things count	136. big things come.
137. Harmony	137. within your heart	137. to touch others.
138. Enough miracles	138. around you.	138. see with the inner eye.
139. forward march	139. with simple soundness	139. give good energy.
140, look carefully	140. with every glance.	140. notice your blessings.
141. You are a light	141. create your environment	141. the debris is hidden treasure.
142. Every day you realize.	142. more and more.	142. LIFE changes.
143. Stand up	143, wherever you're needed.	143. you make the difference.
144. Fool's gold is hard	144. stay with real treasure	144. your heart's true reckonin
145. Faith returns	145. in strange ways	145. with strangers.
146. The good	146. It's confusing	146. patience is the key.
147. Ask a tree	147. to help	147. watch response.
148. Tomorrow	148. surprises	148. along the way.
149. Get simple	149. Answer calmly.	149. remain loving.
150. Everything	150. clears up.	150. all problems shine.
151. Your unique approach	151. new idea	151. success imminent.
152. Pressures	152. create	152. solution to worry.
153. Play a new game	153. To find a new reward	153. totally unexpected.

Customized Fortunes

#154-180

154. Find freedom	**154.** within	154. your own sphere.
155. Where ever you go	155. luck is with you	155. do your best.
156. Pleasures	156. sweep away doubts.	156. Enjoy
157. Everything	157. is magical	157. with focus
158. Classy behavior	158. around the clock	158. no regrets.
159. Finish the project.	159. pertinent info.	159. on vacation.
160. Old message	160. slow down a bit.	160. deal with the reality.
161. A simple meeting	161. brings happiness.	161. empty your mind.
162. Old fashioned ways	162. attract	162. people respond.
163. Rewarding experiences	163. They come to you	163. without a struggle.
164. Lots of sleep	164. in due time	164. flash of inspiration.
165. Take a new road	165. sunny days	165. energy returns..
166. Hop on a plane	166. skip the anxiety.	166. Jump start happiness.
167. Don't droop the issue.	167. Clear up misunderstandings	167. Persist.
168. Let it pass.	168. Avoid nothing.	168. accepting is creating.
169. It's a formula	169. break the mold	169. gold inside.
170. Test your theory	170 don't fear results	170 have passion.
171. Blessings blossom	171. your safety net	171. for a good life.
172. Balance	172. your pleasure arises	172. with high values
173. Each day	173. A different arena	173. for new possibilities.
174. Real treasure	174. gather riches	174. with noble words.
175. Joy is knitted	175. from modest materials	175. all around you.
176. Slow down	176. don't pass up the minute	176. It will change your life.
177. Your needs are met	177. skip to the solution.	177. inner whispers.
178. Keep your cool.	178. Go to school.	178. You're no fool.
179. You know answers	179. without questions	179. Intuitively
180. Pitch your product	180 Wherever you look	180. Confidence returns.

Customized Fortunes

#181-207

181. let regrets vanish
182. Your choice
183. Be different today
184. Hold back words
185. Fine as you are
186. Help is on the way
187. Roller coaster
188. Close the deal
189. Remember who you are
190. Unbelievable event
191. Look for an omen
192. Coincidental meeting.
193. It's coming to a head
194. Whatever your need
195. There's magic here.
196. It takes concentration.
197. Please yourself first
198. Whether or not you know
199. Seek adventure.
200. Restless heart
201. Lifted heart
202. Enough excuses
203. If you're a believer.
204. Don't forget.
205. Sing praises
206. Depend upon it.
207. When you finish

181. let there be light
182. Perféct present idea.
183. Follow hunches
184. Fortunate events
185. climb your mountain
186. don't get involved
187. hang in there
188. snip, snap, done
189. let go
190. materializes
191. wish is corroborated
192. Happiness ensues
193. keep your eyes open
194. Ask again and again
195. Perception shapes invisible.
196. Understand the force.
197. Take a first step.
198. get off the bandwagon
199. coping is not the answer
200. love is coming.
201. think again
202. Life is flowing.
203. let others help
204. mission is possible
205. your heart gets lighter
206. Pleasant days.
207. you will know reason

181. Let Life lead you.
182. Feel your pulse rise.
183. in every instant.
184. advance quickly.
185. resulting in victory.
186. jobs are available
187. swift justice.
188. cash and carry.
189. shoo the beasts away.
190. unsought blessing.
191. and your faith restored
192. new action by you.
193 for several days.
194. someone fulfills you.
195. Imagination unfolds miracles.
196. Don't underestimate.
197. Friends & Lovers
198. whistle your own tune.
199. Monitor what you say.
200. Dejá vu.
201. Reminders give choice.
202. Play with the toys.
203. God guides you.
204. you are in winning circle.
205. And it's the perfect moment
206. Favors all around.
207. Life is worthwhile.

Customized Fortunes

#208-216

208. Get ready to win	208. with wishes	208. Make further attempts.
209. Best way to start	209. with confidence	209. along the route.
210. Patience holds the key.	210. Opens doors.	210. destiny's there.

BONUS CUSTOM FORTUNES

211. Do yourself a favor.	211. then you'll believe	211. Examine dynamics.
212. Company coming	212. Don't be jealous	212. rise above negatives
213. Shop around	213. But don't be gullible.	213. Expect two miracles this month
214 Relax your mood	214. Keep mind clear	214. Mood changes.
215. Be Rich - Chew well	215. any time	215. Go do it.
216. Come to a better view	216. Clues will come	216. P.S. God loves you.

MORE POSSIBILITIES to increase the total

1. In any column, read three phrases, one under the other.
2. Switch numbers around for the next question.
3. Choose 2 numbers from Column 1 and one from Column 2.
4. Reverse using 2 from column 2 and 1 from column 1.
5. Then use the first and third columns in the same way.
6. Use the second and third columns similarly.
7. Use a single column for all 3 choices.
8. Use only one answer from any column.
9. Use one word by itself or in combinations.
10. Feeling blue? Without asking anything, let your eye wander up and down, across columns through pages reading all necessary answers,until satisfied.

Yes you can get 16,000,000 or more interesting and meaningful fortunes. This amount doubles when you consider that each question is a factor in the combination. The same answer to another question is another fortune.

Sweet Dreams

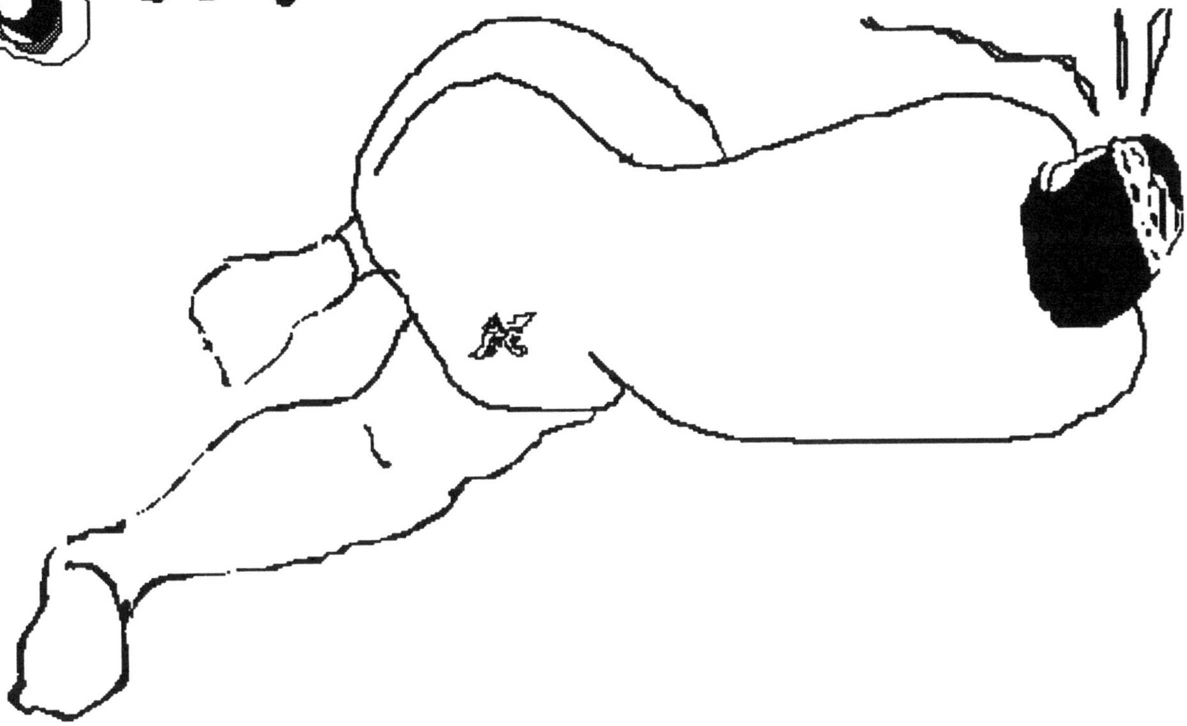

OASIS SEVEN: SONGS

Songs are made to sweep away worries
Songs are made to change worry's tune
But you must sing songs loudly, clearly
In the Morning, Night and Afternoon.

It's El nino - head for shore.

LET THE WIND BLOW

LET THE WIND BLOW

LET THE WIND BLOW

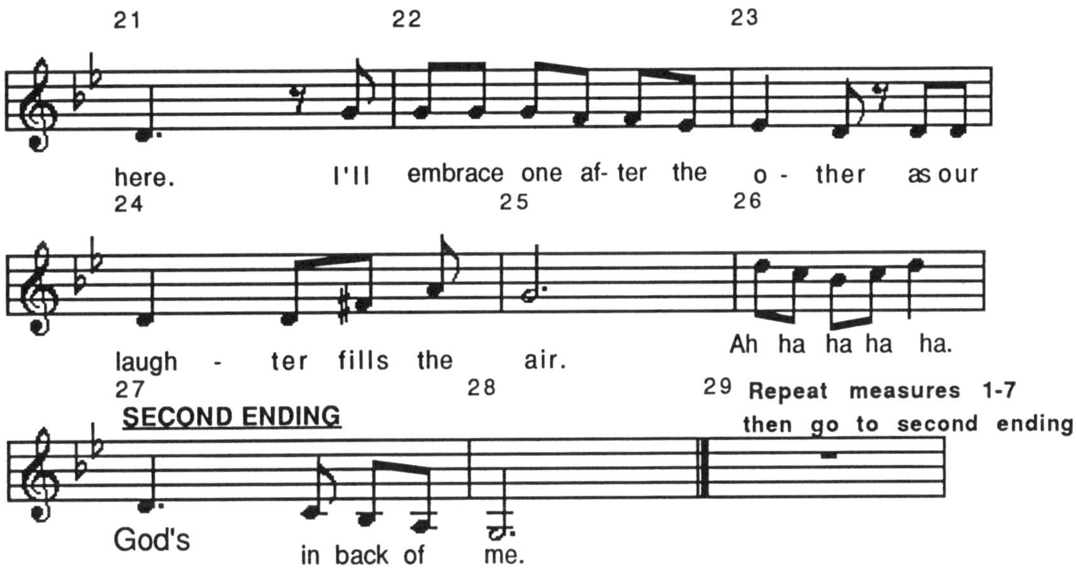

"When life's winds are strong, be ready with a song and you win over all obstacles."

SONGS: Vitamins E, L, B. Energy, Love, Buoyancy

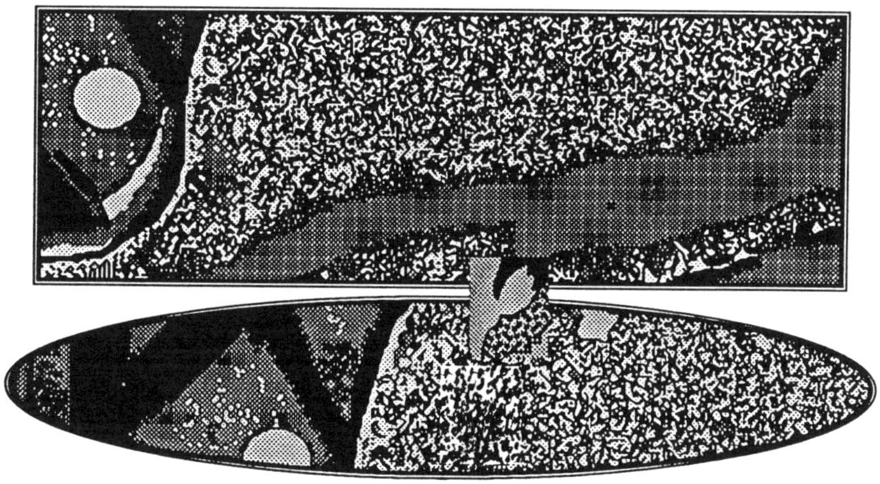

Fortune Song: THE BOTTOM LINE

Words & Music ©1997 Sheindeleh

Love is at the top

How long you plan to stay down there honey? Are you ever coming up?

The bottom line is money

Review your life. Subtle changes will lead you up to a new and rewarding career Put your eyes on the mountain and climb

THE BOTTOM LINE

Words & Music ©1997 Sheindel[illegible]

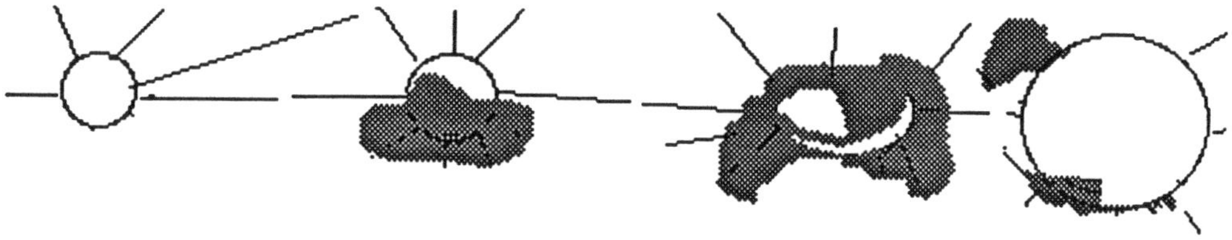

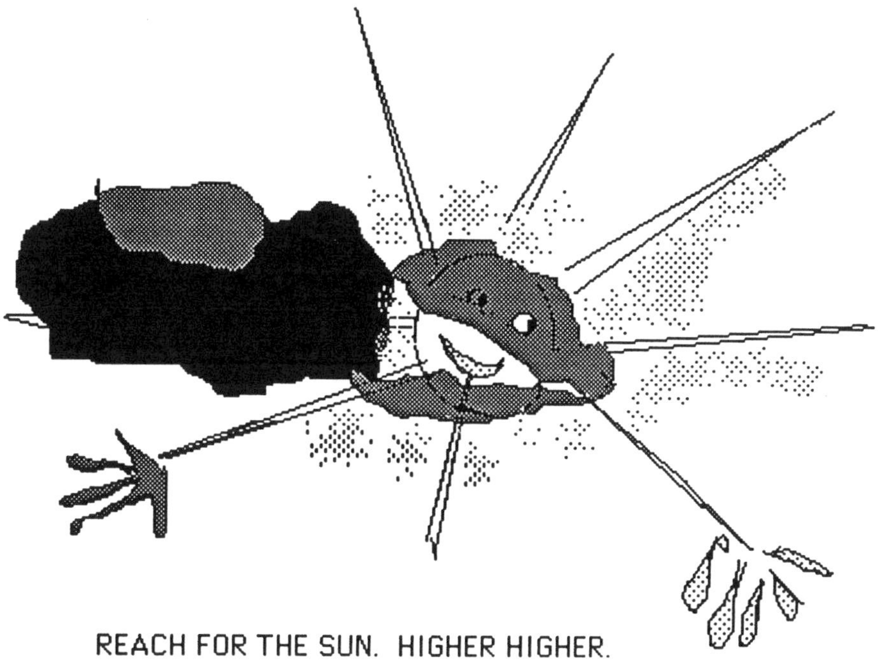

REACH FOR THE SUN. HIGHER HIGHER.

Drawing by Sheindeleh ©1997

REACH FOR THE SUN

Words & Music ©1997 Sheindeleh

SKY
from ground to light years
©1997 Sheindeleh

SKY

Art, Inner Words & Outer Music ©1997 Sheindeleh

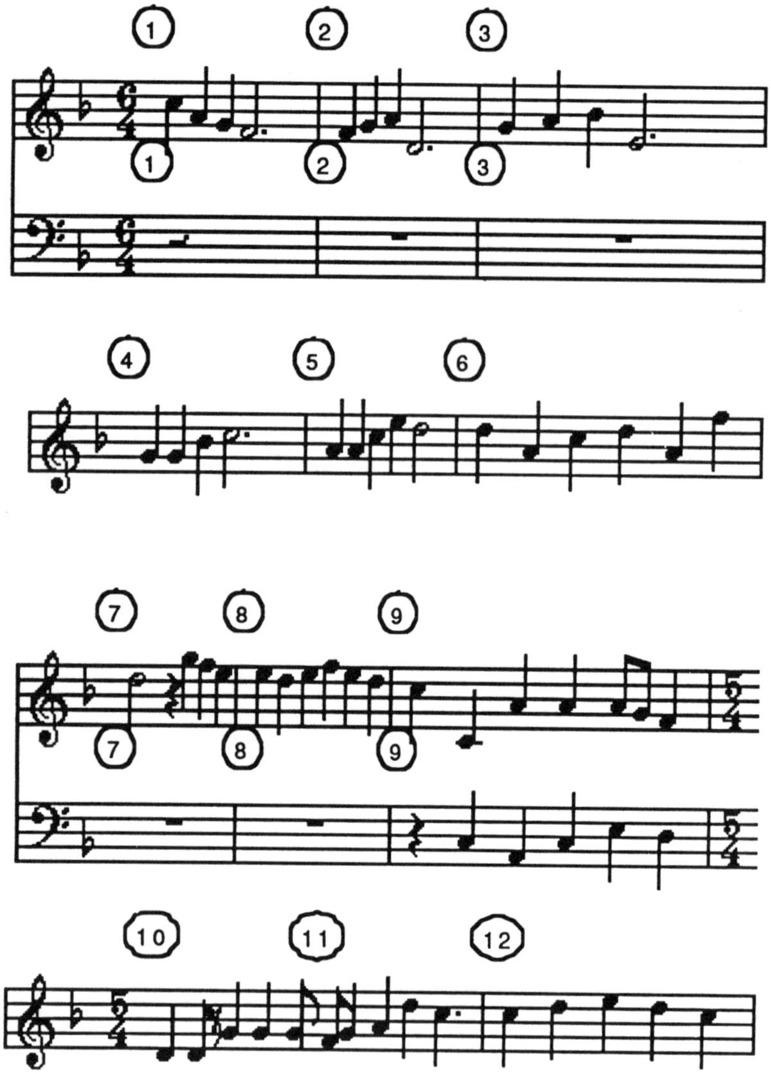

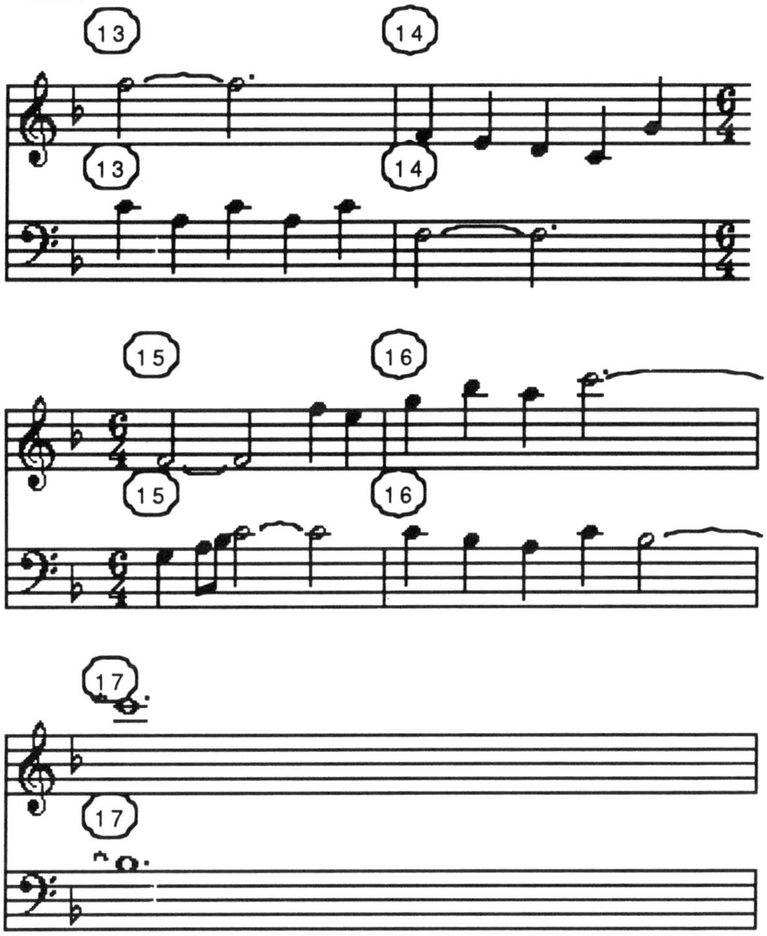
13
14
13
14
15
16
15
16
17
17

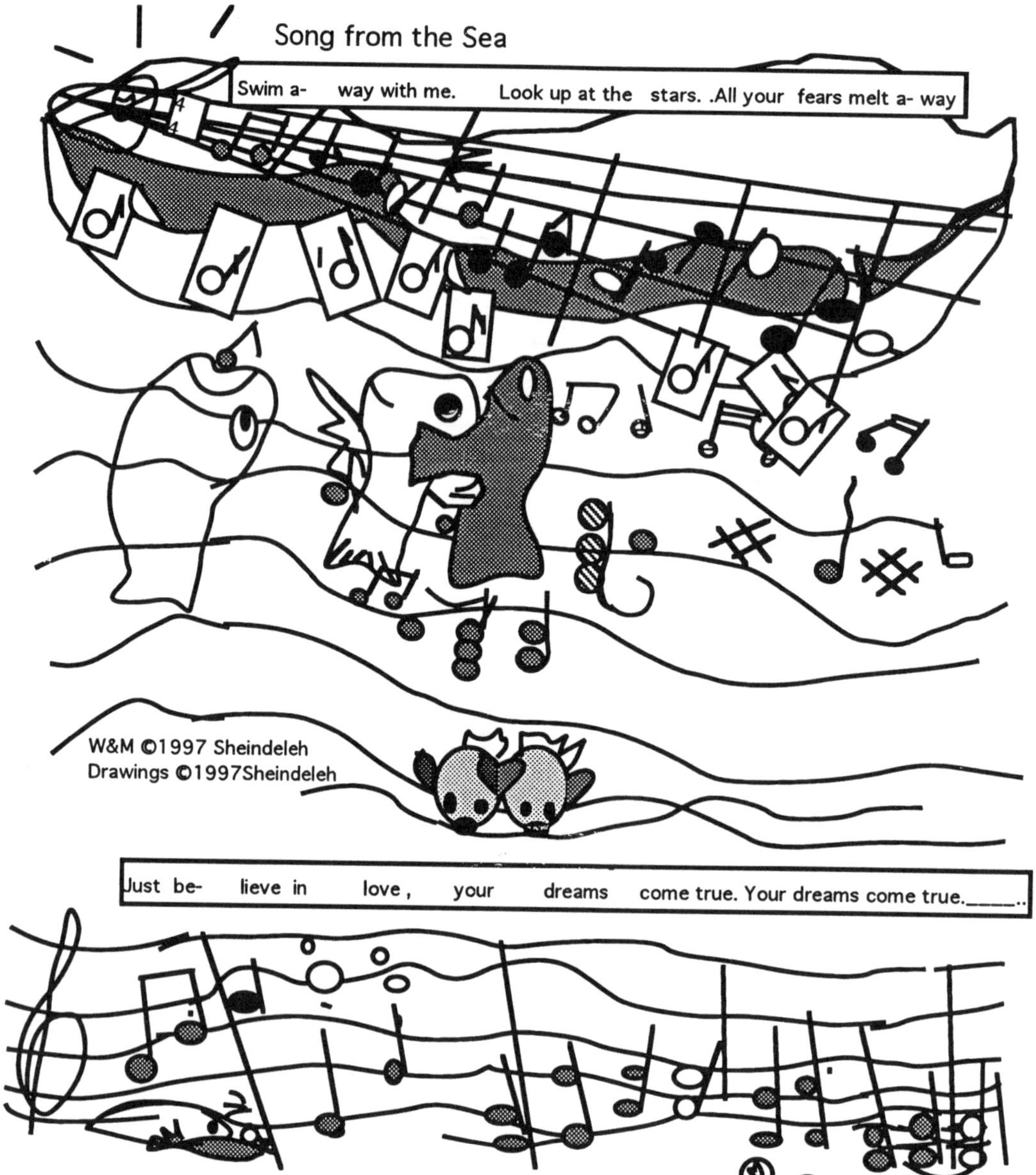

SONG FROM THE SEA
Swim away with me
Look up at the stars
All your tears melt away
Just believe in love,
Your dreams come true,
Your dreams come true.

"Rescue your thoughts from drowning in tears. Throw out a net of self-love."

Drawing ©1997 Sheindeleh

WITH INFINITE INTELLIGENCE

Journeys seemingly impossible at base line, are accomplished when one takes steps and foregoes worry.

The idea: IMPOSSIBLE!

<u>Its accomplishment: INCREDIBLE!!</u>

YOU'LL MEET SOMEONE YOU LOVE TODAY

A Fortune Song: Words & Music ©1997 Sheindeleh

A Fortune Song

You'll Meet Someone You Love Today

Words & Music ©1997 Sheindeleh

* Too high? Try it an octave lower.

A Fortune Song

You'll Meet Someone You Love Today — **Words & Music ©1997 Shirley Goldstein**

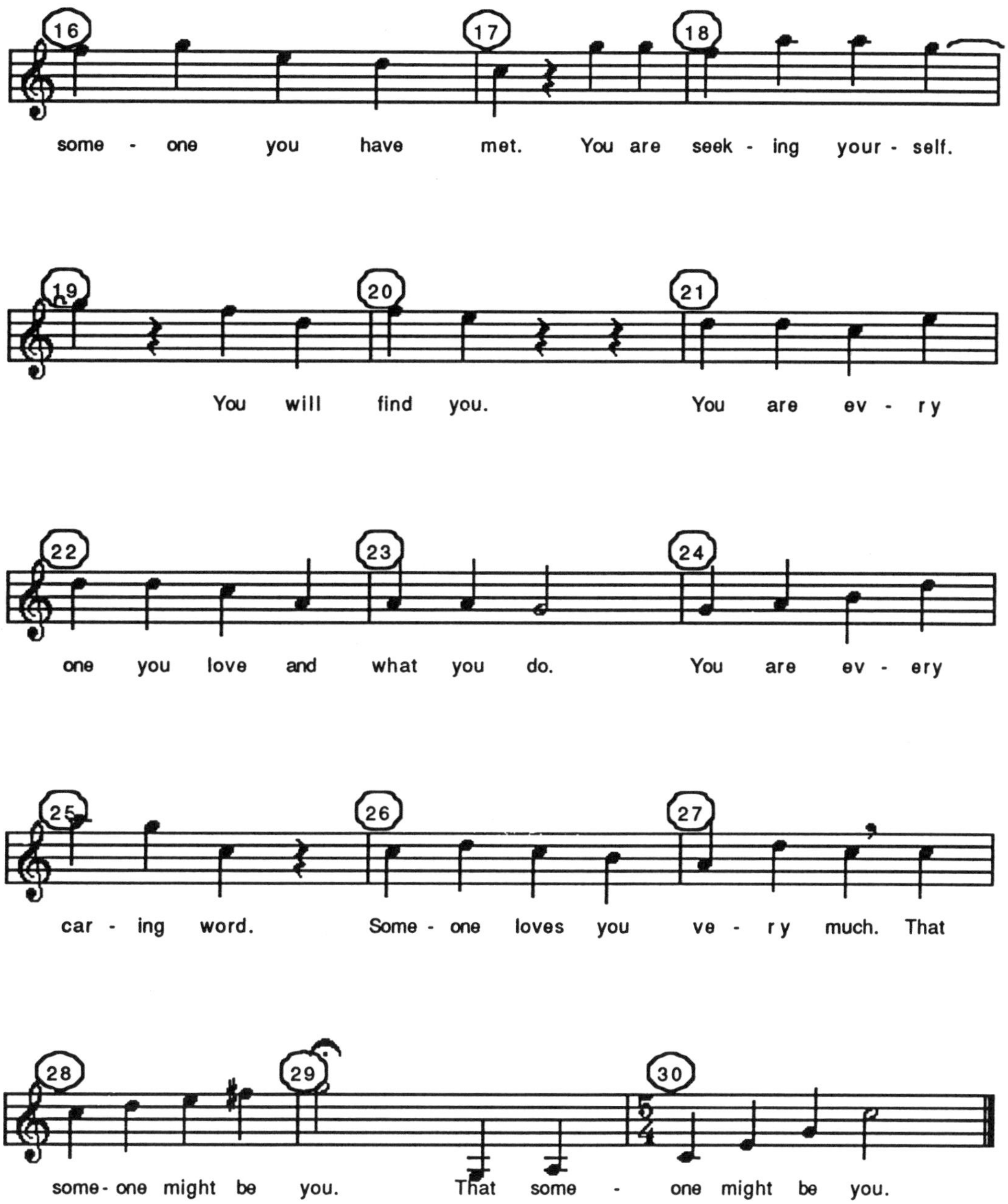

Fortune Saver
©1997 Sheindeleh

Fortune Saver
©1997 Sheindeleh

Fortune Saver ©1997 Sheindeleh

PASTE YOUR FAVORITES HERE

PASTE NEEDED FORTUNES HERE

Paste answered prayers here.

AND YOU ALWAYS HAVE A FRIEND

They will lead you to good life.

They will remind you that prayer works.

MOTHER EARTH

ANAGRAM: MOTHER: EARTH:
OM HERT HEART

Take care of the Mother. She takes care of you.
She is ailing and needs tender care. Take care of the Mother who nurtures us all.

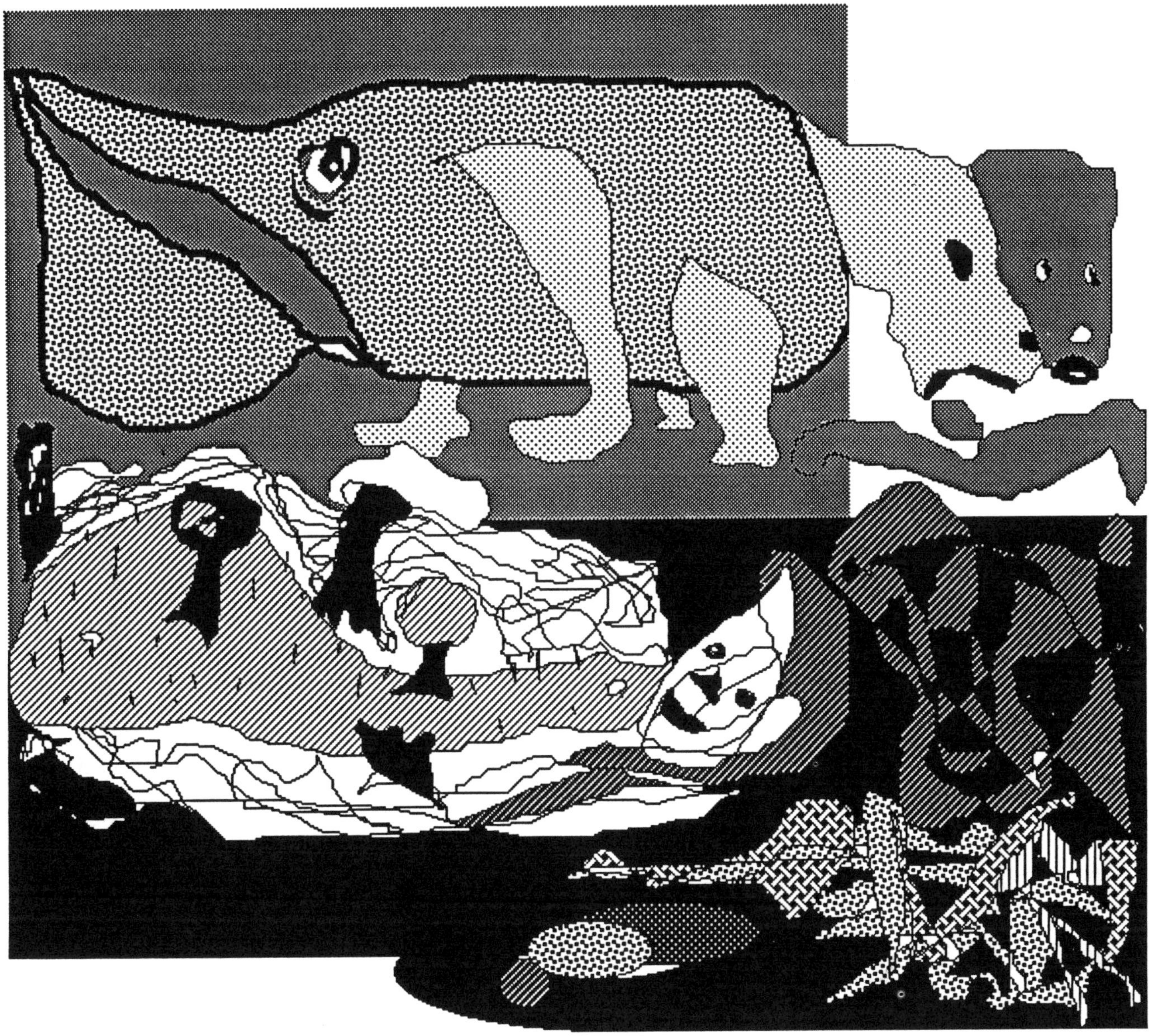

OASIS 8
Back Matter

Offers,gifts, and good-bys.

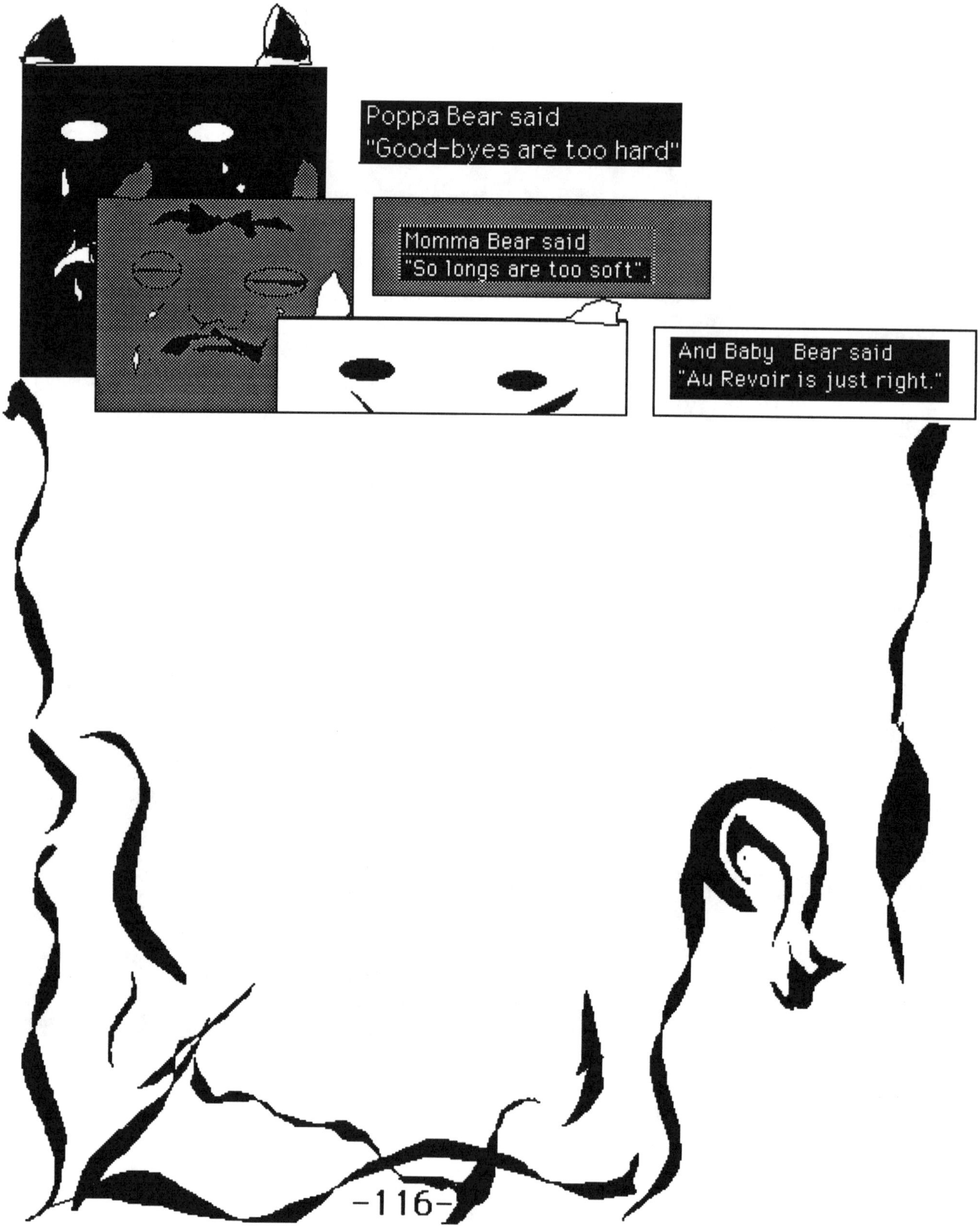
Poppa Bear said
"Good-byes are too hard"
Momma Bear said
"So longs are too soft".
And Baby Bear said
"Au Revoir is just right."

GOOD-BYE FOR NOW

It was full of joy and so on. Before is now.
I leave you in good hands... your own.
To continue the journey. Continue is what
we do. So much to say to you. Etc. Etc.

Sheindeleh April 3, 1998

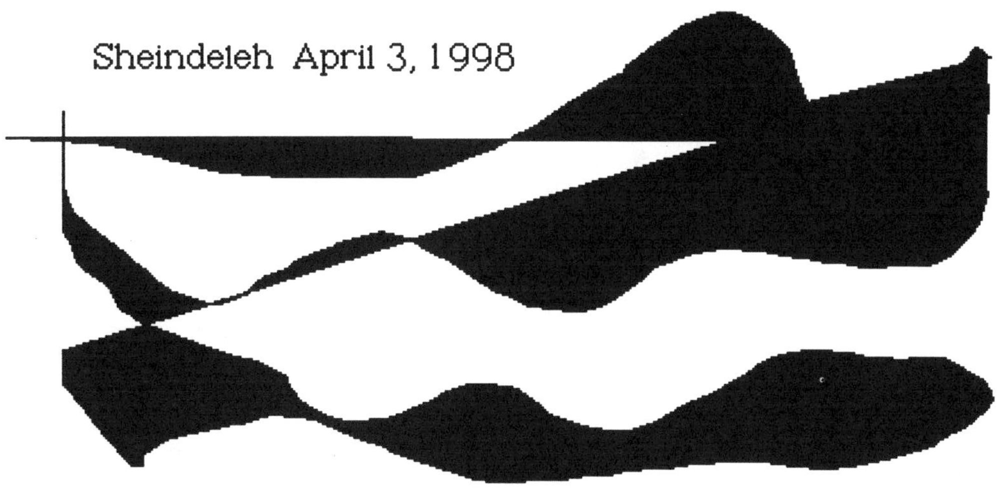

THERE ARE TWO MAZES. **Revive your energy by going through one or both.**

Outside you can imagine a maze and walk through it several times.

Build a maze growing flowers around its perimeters. Close your eyes and let the smell lead you into the center.

Fortune Saver

Fortune Writers

Fortune Writers

WRITE FORTUNES

YOUR HEART SINGS.

Take dictation from G-d & write.

YOU KNOW WHERE TO SCRATCH

WRITE THE NOTES TO HEAR YOUR SONG

It reminds you God speaks to you

...ORDER PAGE...

OTHER BOOKS IN THE MAKING

If you'd like to know when the next book is out
send a Self Addressed Stamped envelope to:

Each book is enclosed in a Sea through print drawstring bag (no string)
and is free while supplies last.

Colorful opaque fabric drawstring bag $5 each

If ordering with books shipping is free (1 per ea. book)

If ordering separately (1-5 bags) include $3 shipping.

Optional: FTG glue design (you color w/markers).

ORDER FORM FORTUNES TO GO

NAME____________________________

ADDRESS____________________________

CITY____________________________

STATE________________ ZIP__________

	QTY.	PRICE	TOTAL	SHIPPING
SOFT COVER	_____	@ $20	_____	_____
HARD COVER	_____	@ $25	_____	_____
fabric DRAWSTRING BAG	_____	@ $ 5.	_____	_____

Yes I wish the glue design ☐

No send me the plain fabric bag ☐

SHIPPING CHARGES:

Paperbk.	Hardcover
1 - $3	1 - $3
2 - $3	2 - $4
3 - $4	3 - $6

Additional books will be sent in separate boxes at same rate.

NOTE: For hard & soft cover mix use shipping price of hard cover book.

Total Shipping _____

SUBTOTAL________

NYS tax(____%) ________

GRAND TOTAL________

MAKE CHECKS PAYABLE TO **ESTMOR PRESS**

Estmor Press - P.O. Box 10985 - Staten Island, N. Y. 10301- 1432

Allow 2-4 weeks from date received for delivery.

<u>When you've tried your best and it gets worse</u>
<u>Remember this:</u>

1. Crisis is over
   before you know what hit you.

2. Your leap to success is coming. Fasten your seat
   belt.

3. Transfer half your assets from brain to heart.

4. Periodic sanity break over due Take one.

5. If you blew it,
   light another candle.

6. Time for a break shake.
   Mix yourself with outside air.
   Shake head well, look up at the sky
   Watch the birds go by
   Say hello to a tree or to me
   and don't think. If overdosed with relief
   Smile and exhale.